D1565400

THE PREACHER
AND THE NEW
ENGLISH BIBLE

THE PREACHER AND THE NEW ENGLISH BIBLE

by

Gerald Kennedy

NEW YORK
OXFORD UNIVERSITY PRESS
1972

THIS IS FOR HALFORD E. LUCCOCK
OF BLESSED MEMORY

CONTENTS

FOREWORD

In the latter part of the nineteenth century a German pastor and scholar, Adolf Deissmann, was on a visit to a friend in Marburg. There he found a volume of Greek papyri from Egypt. Looking through this publication, he was struck by the similarity between its vocabulary and construction and that of the New Testament. He began to study other common documents, and he found that *koine,* the Greek language of the common man, was the language of the New Testament. The man who regarded that language as the speech of the Holy Spirit spoke more profoundly than he knew. For God does not speak to men in academic language, but in the common speech of their everyday experience.

The Bible, of course, is the Christian's guidebook. It is not to be kept on a shelf and dusted regularly; it is to be picked up and read, at any time of the day or night. When I was in Israel I found that the Bible in that country is a book of geography and travel, to be used as one would use a contemporary guide to the country. This is the style of the New English Bible.

The Bible is primarily the Christian preacher's book, and when our preaching ceases to be biblical, it ceases to be relevant. If preaching in our time has fallen upon bad days, it is partly because we have been looking for substitutes for the Book. People do get tired of hearing editorials and commentaries on current events from the pulpit when they do not sense that a man with a deep understanding of the Bible is speaking to them.

I have not aimed at presenting sermons for my fellow preachers, but only at providing a spark which may set their minds aflame. Such sparks may come from a conversation, a newspaper story, a billboard, a book, a personal experience, or the New English Bible.

It is my hope that any Christian will find stimulation and inspiration herein. I never fail to find some fresh insight when I read the New English Bible, no matter how familiar the passage. If the commentary on a particular verse fails to strike fire, then the sheer drama and excellence of the translation itself will do it. Katherine Mansfield, in her *Journal,* wrote about discovering the Bible in her mature life. She had not read it when she was young. She was in one of her periodic exiles, living in the mountains, fighting her losing battle against tuberculosis. "I feel so bitterly that I never have known these facts before," she writes. "They ought to be part of my very breathing." To which I simply conclude, Amen!

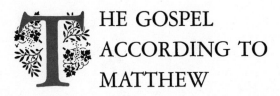

THE GOSPEL ACCORDING TO MATTHEW

INTRODUCTION

> "Do not suppose that I have come to abolish the Law and the prophets; I did not come to abolish, but to complete." 5:17

This gospel was probably written between A.D. 70 and 115. We are not sure who the author was, though traditionally he was the disciple Matthew. We are sure that he was a man steeped in the Old Testament and that he regarded the gospel as a new law and the church as a new Israel. The church has always been urged by some Christians to cut itself off from the Old Testament. Marcion, in the early part of the second century A.D., wanted a complete separation between Jesus' word of love and the Old Testament's word of law. The church has been given grace enough to perceive this proposition as a heresy.

Matthew's understanding is in harmony with science's later discovery of the orderly universe. Roger Bacon said in the thirteenth century: "I will conduct my experiments on the magnetic forces of the lodestone at the selfsame shrine where my fellow-scientist, St. Francis, performed his experiments on the magnetic forces of love." To a Christian this is one world, and Matthew stands as a strong witness to the eternal truth of moral law. There are not many subjects on which we have such a clear and direct answer from Jesus as we do in the case of the reality of law.

Matthew's gospel also teaches us the importance of our heritage. We stand on the shoulders of men who have gone before us, and we have no justification for the conceit we show in our claim to being self-made men. The grandmother who was determined never to take an airplane trip said, "Not me. Flying is against human nature. I am staying here on earth watching television as the Lord intended I should do." Well, she was not entirely wrong. We take what comes to us and we appropriate what is useful. But no man starts with a fresh sheet, and all of us have inherited much from those before us.

Finally, Matthew brings us the good news of obligation and responsibility. We have a debt to the past as well as to the future, and while we often resent the burdens of obligation and duty, without them our life lacks joy and satisfaction. Edward Gibbon, when he had finished the long hard labor of writing *The Decline and Fall of the Roman Empire,* commented that at first he felt released. But then he added, "My pride was soon humbled and a sober melancholy was spread over my mind by the idea that I had taken an everlasting leave of an old and agreeable companion." We find that a sense of obligation and responsibility is a good traveling companion. We preach the good news that we follow One who did not come to abolish the Law and the prophets, but to complete them.

WHAT'S YOUR HURRY?

> There were thus fourteen generations in all from Abraham to David, fourteen from David until the deportation to Babylon, and fourteen from the deportation until the Messiah. 1:17

Matthew gives us a genealogy which begins with Abraham. Is it proper to think of our Lord as coming like a bolt from the blue? Not according to Matthew, for to him cutting off the New Testament from the Old Testament was unthinkable. That would cut us off from all those generations who were the channel through which God gave his Son to the world.

We are in a hurry, but God is not. In March of 1967, in eastern Canada, an eleven-year-old boy died of old age. He was the victim of a rare and strange disease called *progeria* — advanced aging. Senility, hardened arteries, baldness, and slack and wrinkled skin are the marks of the disease. This child lived a lifetime of biological change in his eleven years. Modern high technological societies show this peculiar ailment. They are old and worn out before they have really lived, because the speed of change has mesmerized them. Change has become an end in itself.

To the Jews of ancient times the important thing was to recognize the Messiah when he appeared. But the generation of the first century failed to see who Jesus was. Above all, let us of the twentieth century see that God is the Lord of Time and that His mighty purposes can neither be delayed nor hurried. Christians are saved from the "future shock" which a modern writer describes as the prevailing sickness of our time.

REPENT RIGHT NOW

> About that time John the Baptist appeared as a preacher in the Judean wilderness; his theme was: "Repent; for the kingdom of Heaven is upon you!"
>
> 3:1

Every preacher needs a theme, and John the Baptist rang the changes on one great word: repent. Whatever his particular sermon was about, it would end with this urgent word, that the kingdom was upon them and the generation must repent to receive it. Much modern preaching has no theme. It comments this week on the latest news, and next week it changes to center on some passing headline. One criticism many laymen make is that their preachers do not bring them a word over and beyond what they read in the newspaper. There was an old lady who was asked by a neighbor what the preacher's subject was going to be on Sunday. She replied, "What his particular subject will be is not so very important. You can be sure that he will be telling us the good news of Jesus Christ in the sermon."

The gospel is inexhaustible. The student preacher, thinking of all the sermons he must preach, becomes frightened. But the older preacher, sensing the shortness of life, is concerned that he will not have time to explore all the themes demanding expression.

Running through the gospel is a sense of action demanded *now*. Do not dawdle over it, "for the kingdom of Heaven is upon you." No time to waste, for it is at the door. The old American folk hymn caught the spirit:

> Go tell it on the mountain,
> Over the hills and everywhere,
> Go tell it on the mountain
> That Jesus Christ is born.

WILDERNESS CRYING FOR A VOICE

> It is of him that the prophet Isaiah spoke when he said, "A voice crying aloud in the wilderness, Prepare a way for the Lord; clear a straight path for him." 3:3

If John was a voice crying in the wilderness, the wilderness was crying for a voice. Men wander through the unknown and become lost. But the preacher in the church is a voice speaking to the confused and troubled.

We want a voice giving direction. The changing orders of our experience are too confusing for us to find our way through them. We try something new with great enthusiasm and wake up one day to discover that we have simply circled back to where we were. Progress becomes a mirage and we are in need of someone who can see farther.

We need a voice of hope. When Dante, in his *Divine Comedy,* inscribed over the entrance to hell, "Abandon hope all ye who enter here," he described many a life. Any man who has had hopeless periods engulf him knows that Dante's words are a good definition of hell. As a young woman said to her psychiatrist, "Doctor, I need something to look forward to." So do we all, and the voice of the church is one of hope.

We cry out for a voice giving meaning to the human venture. Despair comes not because the going is hard, but because we doubt that the going means anything. Christians are not forerunners of the Christ, they are His followers. And they are voices that turn the wilderness into a highway.

ON WHOM HIS FAVOR RESTS

> ... and a voice from heaven was heard saying, "This is my Son, my Beloved, on whom my favour rests."
>
> 3:17

Here is the source of Jesus' authority. God's favor rested upon him. I had a professor once who troubled me by what he said, because it was so foreign to what I had accepted. But I never doubted that when he spoke I was listening to a man who had a true knowledge of God. The Christian has this quality when God finds him. The preacher has it when his study and devotion have led him into the knowledge of the Almighty. This is a serious lack of some modern preachers and much contemporary preaching. An old colleague said to me, when I was elected to my present office, "Young man, you will have only as much authority as you deserve, no matter what the *Discipline* says." Until God's favor rests upon us we can never find the authoritative word no matter how many degrees we have earned. Authority is a quality which springs from knowledge of God.

CURE OF SOULS

> He went round the whole of Galilee...curing whatever illness or infirmity there was among the people.
>
> 4:23-24

This is the pastoral ministry! Jesus touched people wherever they were, and to whatever need they had, He ministered. Some of those diseases He healed were physical in origin; probably most of them were mental and spiritual. No special group for Him; He ministered to "whatever illness or infirmity there was among the people." A good word for men who think that they are called to serve in just certain places and to minister just to certain kinds of people.

One of the great responsibilities and privileges of ministers has been called "The Cure of Souls." Today we call it counseling, but the old designation is rich in meaning. Our bodies, our minds, and our spirits are so much of a piece that we must think of Christian healing as restoring the person to wholeness.

Bishop William Taylor traveled the world over as an evangelist. The climax of his meetings was a call for tithers—a strange climax for a revival meeting. But Taylor believed that unless a man committed his money he was not truly cured spiritually. The ministry of Jesus was directed toward curing "whatever illness or infirmity there was among the people." Sometimes that illness is a lack of generosity.

WHAT WE NEED MOST

> "How blest are those who know their need of God...."
>
> 5:3

To say that the great need of modern man is to worship God sounds totally irrelevant to some. Yet the common human disease is lack of direction, lack of focus, and lack of a conviction. Most of the diseases of men spring from this particular one.

Carl Jung wrote, in *Modern Man in Search of a Soul:* "During the past thirty years people from all the civilized countries of the earth have consulted me. I have treated many hundreds of patients, the larger number being Protestants, a small number of Jews, and not more than five or six believing Catholics. Among all my patients in the second half of life—that is to say, over thirty-five—there has not been one whose problem in the last resort was not that of finding a religious outlook on life. It is safe to say that every one of them fell ill because he had lost that which the living religions of every age have given to their followers, and none of them have been really healed who did not regain his religious outlook. This, of course, had nothing whatever to do with a particular creed or membership of a church." Jesus says this in the first beatitude.

TO SEE RIGHT PREVAIL

> "How blest are those who hunger and thirst to see right prevail; they shall be satisfied."   5:6

The familiar word is "righteousness," but how much sharper to say that we must hunger and thirst to see the right win. If we hunger and thirst for it, we will be driven to personal commitment to the causes of right. We will not be satisfied to lose ourselves in some vague hope that righteousness should be done. We will be actively on the side of the right wherever it becomes apparent to us. That would not be a bad definition of a Christian: a man who is utterly committed to helping the right prevail.

HYPOCRISY IN REVERSE

> "I tell you, unless you show yourselves far better men
> than the Pharisees and the doctors of the law, you
> can never enter the kingdom of Heaven."   5:20

Hypocrisy often goes into reverse. We talk about being worse
than we are and we lean over backwards insisting that we are
not saints. This demand that we must be "far better men" at
first startles us. It brings us face to face with one of the chief
weapons the Christian has in his armory. John Wesley told men
to aim for perfection. It is still an embarrassment to young
preachers entering a United Methodist Conference to be asked
if they expect to be made perfect in love. The boys stutter on
that one. Yet Wesley was quite in harmony with this word from
the Sermon on the Mount. Our warfare demands superiority of
life. Even so, we are saved from pride by the gap between what
we aim for and what we achieve. The saint never knows he is
a saint, and the good man is never aware of his goodness, but
neither one should be ashamed to make goodness his goal.

Behold a mystery. The better a man becomes, the more
humble he is. For he never gains enough to be proud. He always
finds his shelter in the perfection of Jesus Christ. But he is
saved from taking comfort from aiming low and being content
with just average behavior.

STOP SNEERING

> "If he abuses his brother he must answer for it to the
> court; if he sneers at him he will have to answer for it
> in the fires of hell."   5:22

When we sneer we lift ourselves high by reducing another man
to something less than one for whom Christ died. All sympathy
is gone and the self-satisfied brother tries to belittle other men.
Sneering is of the devil.

The scholar who sneers at the uneducated and naïve is condemned.

The well-to-do who sneers at the poor man carrying the burden of his poverty is judged.

The comfortable who looks with ill-concealed contempt on the loathesomeness of the sick is in danger of "the fires of hell."

We ought to form the habit of praying for every man we meet who is in any distress. This will cure us of sneering.

NO NEED FOR ELABORATION

> "Plain 'Yes' or 'No' is all you need to say; anything beyond that comes from the devil."   5:37

The old farmer, listening to a local politician, was asked what he thought of the campaign speech. "Well," said the old man, "he talks considerably like I do when I'm lying." Nothing is more refreshing than to hear the plain speech of a plain man speaking the plain truth. This is eloquence far beyond our contriving. Our Lord wiped out all elaborate oaths men used to show their sincerity. The Friends set us an example with their plain speech and their unadorned rhetoric. Christians are to be men of plain yes and plain no. This is a good word for preachers.

John A. Rice, whose uncle was a Methodist Bishop, said this about his uncle's preaching: "To listen to him was like quietly getting drunk. He led his hearers by easy stages into an unreal world of effortless peace, drugging them gradually into unconsciousness by the melody that was himself. They went home to eat their Sunday dinners in dazed silence and remain befuddled until Monday morning, when they woke up and went about their business."

BE EXTRAORDINARY

> "And if you greet only your brothers, what is there
> extraordinary about that?"   5:47

Christians think they do well if they do the ordinary things
which morality demands. Here is Jesus' demand: his followers
must be "extraordinary." One of our greatest failures is that we
are just run-of-the-mill people. Church members are little
different from the other citizens of the world.

The early Christians impressed people because they were
extraordinary. The evangelistic power of the early Christian
groups lay in their extraordinariness. Let me try another definition of Christians: people whose personal relationships and
ideas always have an extraordinary quality.

G. K. Chesterton, in *The Notebook,* which he kept from
1894 to 1899, wrote: "Once I found a friend. 'Dear me,' I said,
'he was made for me.' But now I find more and more friends
who seem to have been made for me, and more and yet more
made for me. Is it possible we were all made for each other all
over the world?" Now there is an extraordinary idea for you!

STOP BABBLING

> "In your prayers do not go babbling on like the
> heathen, who imagine that the more they say the
> more likely they are to be heard."   6:7

Prayers that "go babbling on" is about the best description I
have heard of many public prayers. They give the impression of
a certain amount of time to be filled as the only purpose of the
whole affair. What can cure this?

For one thing, work on public prayers. Public prayers, like
sermons, demand labor. For another thing, let us have something specific in mind when we pray. My old professor told me

to headline somebody I know when I pray. Our prayers should not be so personal as to become sentimental, but someone with actual problems to face and specific burdens to bear ought to be in our minds when we pray. Also, generalities are about as unimpressive in prayer as they are in preaching. For concrete situations and for real human needs, O Lord, help us to pray.

CUT OUT THE GLOOM

> "So too when you fast, do not look gloomy like the hypocrites...."   6:16

Preachers have a lot of fun when they get together. One of the high points of an Annual Conference is the executive session, when only preachers are present and the retiring brethren take a few minutes to speak of their ministries. More people should hear this, for it would change the laymen's picture of the Christian ministry. Preachers have humor that others do not know. Anyone standing outside the church when we are in such a session would think that the brethren had gone crazy. The best stories I hear come from preachers. For the last twenty years the meetings that have brought me the most sheer enjoyment have been the Councils of Bishops. They have been among the most delightful experiences of my life. The days when dyspepsia was mistaken for piety are over, I hope. The Christian has hard fights to win and heavy burdens to carry, but nobody else has quite so much joy. If your religion is not bringing you fun, you are being short-changed. Something is wrong with sad Christians, for gloominess is not the sign of our way of life.

RUSTY AND MOTH-EATEN TREASURES

> "Do not store up for yourselves treasure on earth,
> where it grows rusty and moth-eaten...."   19

What a wonderful description of the treasure of the earth:
"rusty and moth-eaten." How quickly sin grows musty and
dusty. Christ gives us treasures which grow more wonderful
with every passing year and are never corrupted.

Christianity that is full of clichés and pious repetition is really
too earthly. Real Christianity is fresh. The church whose services
are "as usual" has missed the heart of it.

BUSY WORK FOR HEATHEN

> "All these are things for the heathen to run after, not
> for you...."   6:32

Jesus says that these heathen must have something to keep them
busy, and that all their worrying about what to eat, what to
drink, and what to wear accomplishes nothing more. But these
concerns are not for followers of the Way, for God knows what
we need and He provides the necessities. So we may simply
allow the heathen to make too much out of their chase after
these passing amusements and be grateful that we are freed
from it.

NO MASOCHISM, PLEASE

> "Each day has troubles enough of its own."   6:34

Do not add to the burdens which are already heavy enough for
us to carry. Just take it as it comes, a day at a time, and so find
peace of mind and capture the joy with which he expects us to
live.

Masochism is a psychological twist that gives a person pleasure in being abused or dominated. It describes the state of crowding an excessive amount of anxiety into a single day. A wise man said, "I have had many troubles, most of which never actually happened." So many of our troubles are in fear of what might happen. Here are three propositions for the Christian:

1. To live means to have trouble.
2. There is no need to increase trouble by anticipating it.
3. If it arrives God will help us deal with it.

AMEN!

JUDGMENT IS A BOOMERANG

"Pass no judgment, and you will not be judged."
7:1

It is not possible to live without making judgments. We are always exercising this power, because we must. But we should not *deal out* judgments, which is to say, we do not have to *express* them. Putting things into words and discussing conclusions with other people hardens them so they become inflexible. "Pass no judgment" is a good word for us, for then we are able to change our minds.

When a Christian faces a time of judgment he should remember four principles:

1. Most of our conclusions need to have a tentative basis. A man met an acquantance he had labeled in his own mind a "dead-beat." He was startled to hear the fellow say, "By the way, here is that money I owe you." "Keep it," was the reply. "I'd rather go without the money than have to change my mind about you." Changing our judgment should not be that painful.

2. Let us not forget that we believe in the gospel of another chance.

3. Every time we express a judgment we should spend a time

in self-examination. It is well to remember that judgment is a boomerang; instead of hitting the person aimed at, it may circle back and strike the one who threw it.

4. Judgment is one of the things best left to God.

PLANKS AND SPECKS

> "Or how can you say to your brother, 'Let me take the speck out of your eye', when all the time there is that plank in your own?"   7:4

The exaggeration becomes plain in this version. A man with a plank in his eye who dares to give advice about a speck in another man's eye Jesus calls a hypocrite. This is one part of the New Testament which is as modern as tomorrow. With all our preaching the church seems to have too many people still trying to remove specks from the eyes of others without being aware of the planks cutting off their own vision. A wife, a friend, a pastor may help us be cured of this sickness.

A friend sent me a copy of the following he received in the mail: "The objective of all dedicated school employees should be to thoroughly analyze all situations, anticipate all problems prior to their occurence, have answers for these problems, and move swiftly to solve these problems when called upon—however, when you are up to your neck in alligators it is difficult to remind yourself that your initial objective was to drain the swamp."

We very seldom help anybody by complaining of their inadequacies. If they are humble men, they already know about the speck in their eye. If they are not humble men, as most of them are not, it simply causes resentment. They are likely to think to themselves, "Look who's giving the advice. He ought to be taking it instead of giving it." The only way we can help another person is to find some way to ease his burden.

Then it is well for us to remember that if that other man's
vision is inadequate in this instance, ours is no doubt inadequate
in some other realm of human experience. Everybody has blind
spots, and the fellow who is always trying to help his brother
by telling him about his mistakes only cuts himself off from
being of help. We are always over-supplied with people trying
to remove the specks from other people's eyes while there are
planks in their own.

BAD AS YOU ARE

"If you, then, bad as you are, know how to give your
children what is good for them, how much more will
your heavenly Father give good things to those who
ask him!"   7:11

Psychiatrists will raise questions about the parent knowing how
to give children what is good for them. We know how to give
them what we think is good for them, but there are too many
instances of mothers and fathers of good will harming their
children with their generosity. Here we ought to pray for an
understanding of the needs of those we love the most.

I heard a great preacher speak on this text when I was a
student. He called it "Reasoning Up To God." He spoke of
recognizing goodness wherever it appears. If goodness is possible in us, how much greater is the goodness of God?

It is hard for us to grasp the promise of Jesus, that God is
more anxious to give than we are to ask. Once we grasp this,
we are saved.

LONELY ROAD

> "The gate is wide that leads to perdition, there is
> plenty of room on the road, and many go that
> way...."   7:13

This is a good word for a freeway-minded generation. People
want plenty of great wide roads where they can travel fast.
Remember those words of Robert Frost about taking "the one
less traveled by." We should not judge everything by majorities.
Only the poor soul frightened by loneliness, who prefers to be
in a crowd even when it is going in the wrong direction, will be
overly impressed by the wide roads most often traveled. We are
too much influenced by polls and public opinion, and we feel
safer on the road with many other travelers. But man's most
important journeys have to be taken alone. Jesus says that the
narrow untraveled roads and the strait gate are the marks of His
way. The "lonely crowd" does not guarantee pleasant traveling,
and it gives no assurance that the wide road is leading us to
where we want to go. Read again Van Dyke's *The Other Wise
Man.*

There is here an echo of Isaiah's word: "Prepare a road for
the Lord through the wilderness, clear a highway across the
desert for our God" (Isaiah 40:3). Christians should be
pioneers, blazing new trails and clearing new ways. We are
pilgrims. Strange and wonderful sights are most often found
only at the end of the lonely road.

OF COURSE I WILL

> " 'Sir, if only you will, you can cleanse me.' Jesus
> stretched out his hand, touched him, and said,
> 'Indeed I will; be clean again.' "   8:3

This version captures something of the exuberance of Jesus as
he replies to the leper's pleas for healing. The leper says that

Jesus can do it if he will and Jesus' answer is a gracious "Indeed I will." He seems to be saying "Of course I will. You are cleansed."

Christians often let familiarity breed indifference. It even happened to the disciples. We must be men who, first keeping this spirit alive within our own lives and in our own preaching, help to restore to a jaded generation the wonder and miracle of what God has done for us.

ASTONISHED BY FAITH

> Jesus heard him with astonishment, and said to the people who were following him, "I tell you this: nowhere, even in Israel, have I found such faith."
>
> 8:10

Jesus was often disappointed. Many times he found doubt where he might have expected faith. But here, unexpectedly, the father of a sick boy insists that Jesus does not have to come to his home but only to speak a word and his son will be healed. And Jesus "heard him with astonishment." Have you ever met unexpectedly a Christian witness? Or have you ever observed unexpectedly a Christian act? How it lifts up the heart and gives us encouragement! This centurion was one who had the privilege not only of asking for help but of ministering to the Lord. The unexpected word we hear and the unexpected act we observe restores courage and strengthens tired men.

Loren Eiseley, the scientist with the poet's heart, wrote in *The Unexpected Universe* that if we are to see it we must expect it. Even as Jesus found unexpected faith in a Roman soldier, so shall we encounter faith in unexpected places.

SUCH COWARDS

> "Why are you such cowards?" he said; "how little
> faith you have!"   8:26

This is Jesus' word to the frightened disciples when they thought
their boat might go down in the storm. Cowards are people
without faith, and Christians ought to be people with courage
because they have faith. This matter of cowardice haunts us,
but remember that when faith grows weak, so does courage.
The way to heal the coward is to help him with his faith. That
is how the healing of the gospel is experienced.

A lady in Peterborough, England, was on the verge of a
nervous collapse. She insisted that someone kept following her.
No, she did not see him, but she heard footsteps every time she
went for a walk. A doctor at the Peterborough District Hospital
solved the mystery. She was wearing her hearing aid backwards.
What she had thought were footsteps were the sound of her
own heartbeats. When we do not listen to our faith, we turn in
upon ourselves and mistake our fears for realities.

WHO IS INVITED?

> "I did not come to invite virtuous people, but sinners."
> 9:13

Our commission is to the sinners, not to the virtuous. Churches
have a hard time adjusting themselves to the presence of mean
youngsters, unwashed and unattractive. It is not that we so-
called virtuous folks do not need God's presence, it is just that
the churches develop a preference for certain classes of people
and avoid others. A preacher complained to me that his church
ought to move because it was within a half block of a saloon.
I said to him that Jesus would have told him he was right
where he ought to be and that his clientele was right at his own
doorstep.

The church easily turns into a club of people with whom we can feel comfortable. No foreign races and no members of strange classes. One of the best compliments a church ever received came from an observer of the church picnic. "I couldn't make out who they could be," the observer remarked. "They looked such a mixed-up group." That is the church, or at least, that is what it was meant to be by the One who called not the "virtuous people, but sinners."

BEST THINGS ARE FREE

"You received without cost; give without charge."

10:8

This instruction Jesus gave to His disciples, and it remains forever the great missionary and evangelistic commission. It works out in so many parts of life that the song, "The Best Things in Life Are Free," speaks the sober truth.

Arnold Toynbee writes, in *Cities on the Move* (Oxford, 1970): "In the painful material contrast between slums and middle-class residential districts there seems to be a redeeming psychological compensation. The higher the income and the better the roofing and the plumbing, the lower the standard of neighborliness. It is well-known that the poor give to each other far more spontaneous unremunerated mutual aid than the rich give to each other. Indeed, without a high standard of neighborliness, the difficulties and hardships of slum life would be insuperable. The slummier the slum, the higher the standard of neighborliness is apt to be" (p. 227).

But the supreme example of this bounty is what God has done for us in Christ. We did not buy it and we did not deserve it. We should "give without charge."

DO NOT WORRY ABOUT YOUR SPEECH

> "But when you are arrested, do not worry about what
> you are to say...."   10:19

Are we getting back to a time when a valid witness to Christian
values and procedures carries with it the threat of being
arrested? A father told me that his son had been arrested for his
antiwar position. He said that nothing had happened to close
the generation gap so completely as having his own son arrested
for bearing witness to a Christian principle. The early Christians
were familiar with this process, but they did not need to have
special speeches written out for them to give to the authorities.
Jesus said that if a man makes a proper Christian testimony and
is arrested for it, the right words will be given to him.

This is an age of salesmanship. That is where the profits are
so that the youngster is taught to give the right "sales pitch."
Now and again I am cornered by one of these young super-
salesmen. I want to say, "Oh, forget this artificial nonsense. I've
read *How to Win Friends and Influence People.* Just tell me in
a simple, straightforward way what you want." This is always
more effective than clever verbal tricks.

GOD AND THE SPARROWS

> "Are not sparrows two a penny? Yet without your
> Father's leave not one of them can fall to the
> ground."   10:29

Birds have been falling to the ground because of our insecticides
and our pollution of the atmosphere. We have seen pictures of
birds dying because the oil we spilled covers the water. Remember Rachel Carson's *Silent Spring?* Ecology is a great new emphasis, and it is essentially a religious idea. Christian churches
ought to be speaking prophetic words against all so-called
"progress" that we are making at the expense of the environ-

ment. So much of it means the end of our heritage. If we redeem the earth before it is too late, it will be because religious men read the New Testament with new seriousness and see themselves again as disciples of the One who loved the flowers and valued birds.

Theodore Parker wrote in the nineteenth century: "Every rose is an autograph from the hand of God on His world about us. He has inscribed His thoughts in these marvelous hieroglyphics which sense and science have, these many thousand years, been seeking to understand." Said Toyohiko Kagawa, "Science books are letters from God, telling how He runs His universe."

THE BEST SHOW

> "What was the spectacle that drew you to the wilderness? A reed-bed swept by the wind? No? Then what did you go out to see? A man dressed in silks and satins? Surely you must look in palaces for that. But why did you go out? To see a prophet? Yes indeed, and far more than a prophet."   11:7-9

Crowds gather whenever anything unusual is happening. To see John the Baptist the people had to go out of the city, and Jesus comments on what they expected to see when they went out into the wilderness. They went out to hear a prophet, and this passage reflects the warm appreciation Jesus had for his cousin John.

That generation, bad as it was, had a deep hunger for the word of the religious man. They went out to hear John and they came in great crowds to hear Jesus. It was an age similar to ours — irreligious, materialistic, and anti-church. It was also one with a deep hunger for something it had not found, and it was looking for someone to speak about salvation.

The people wanted to hear a prophet who would tell them the truth bluntly, in uncompromising words. When we think of all the tricks that have been worked and the special attractions which have been announced to get people to listen, we conclude that beyond all of these sideshows is the word of a real prophet speaking to his time. This universal hunger of the human heart is something the church always can depend upon and to which it must always speak its word. The blunt word of a good man is more powerful than all the trappings.

The people seek a prophet, for men of all classes want someone to tell them the truth.

HOLY PRAGMATISM

"And yet God's wisdom is proved right by its results."

11:19

We fear that when we deal with religion we are dealing with something that is not provable. Nonsense! God's words are judged by their results, and our final commitment rests upon the assurance that here is something that works. History is the Christian's secular Bible, and experience is every man's university.

The truth of Jesus is revealed both in the young lives that go wrong and in the experiences of the saints. We do not need more authority, but more perception. Sin ends badly and God's way leads men home. Christianity is divine sense and Jesus' teaching is holy pragmatism.

SIMPLE TRUTH

> "...for hiding these things from the learned and wise,
> and revealing them to the simple."   11:25

The Christian is not anti-intellectual when he remembers this verse as a guide for his spirit. The academic, overly complicated approach is common enough and comes from men who know so much that they must qualify every statement. But when they are through, few understand what they mean. There are also men whose wide reading and mystical meditation blinds them to simple fact. The involved approach does not symbolize the deep mind; usually when men speak or write that way, it is because what they are talking about is not clear to them either. How the New Testament shines with illumination when compared with some of the mystics' attempts to put their thoughts into words! Is this because these esoteric brethren have more profound intellects than Jesus? Not so. It simply means that they are having difficulty in communicating.

LIGHTEN YOUR LOAD

> "Come to me, all whose work is hard, whose load is
> heavy; and I will give you relief....For my yoke is
> good to bear, my load is light."   11:28-30

Every man's work is hard and every man's load is heavy. Yet Jesus says we should not to ignore the difficult, as His word is, "For my yoke is good to bear, my load is light." He does not promise to remove the burden, but to make it easier to bear. This is a Christian insight into life. To be free of important tasks should not be our aim. We should find joy in doing something that needs to be done. Dr. Paul Dudley White said that if tension and strain cause heart attacks, he would have had one long ago. Jesus Christ brings to us a new way of life so that the burden is bearable and the load becomes a companion.

This is one of the mysteries of the Christian faith. On the one hand there are its high demands, which seem so formidable to those on the outside. But on the other hand there is this delight in the heart which makes us so full of anticipation that life, as St. Paul said, becomes a pageant. We always go wrong when we try to make our life other than it is or resign ourselves to just doing our duty because it is right. In these great words of our Lord we have the promise that the heavy load becomes bearable and, indeed, amazingly light when we are dedicated to Him. Life in Christ is not a humorless duty, but an exciting adventure. A college girl returned from a blind date and was asked by her roommate, "Well, how did it go?" "I had to slap him six times," was the reply. "Oh, he got fresh?" "No," the girl answered. "I thought he was dead." That is the worst fate. The gospel makes us alive.

THE REAL ISSUE

"And surely a man is worth far more than a sheep!"

12:12

Putting aside all the petty regulations and minutiae of the law, Jesus takes his critics right to the heart of the subject. They would certainly lift a sheep up if it fell into a ditch on the Sabbath. Then how can they be critical of One who heals a human being on the Sabbath? Religion is always in danger of ritual, regulations, and rules which make no sense when the real issue is defined. The bureaucracies of the modern churches often keep us doing the same old thing without reasons simply because they have become traditional. Our Lord always brings us right to the central point and makes us see the human values involved. Then we can draw our own conclusions.

A man must take a fresh look at himself lest his meaningless habits confuse his sense of values. It is too easy to mistake the worth of a sheep with the worth of a man. Longinus pointed out long ago that there is a razor's edge between sublimity and absurdity.

HOPE

" 'In him the nations shall place their hope.' "   12:21

The more we look at the human situation, the more we perceive that hope is the cure for our sicknesses. It is when men lose hope that they do foolish things and bring catastrophe upon their society and themselves. The nation needs hope, and when there is nothing out ahead that calls it forward, it disintegrates in strife and civil conflict. The church needs hope, and it ministers to the people best when it holds before them the great promises God has made. When that vision becomes clouded, life loses its brightness. A man walking along the street saw a litttle girl who kept her eyes on the sidewalk constantly. He overheard her mother ask her, "Why don't you look at the pretty windows, Gracie?" Gracie replied, "I'm looking for something to find." And so are we all! The church which is a center of gloom and pessimism instead of being a place of hope has become a part of the disease instead of part of the healing.

THE REAL ENEMY

> "...unless he has first tied the strong man up before
> ransacking the house?"   12:29

People confuse their friends with their enemies. If you do not
like a fellow you find reasons why he is subversive and dangerous to society. Often if you analyze it you are accusing him of
relationships and representations which are simply foolish if
they are looked at fairly. So Jesus' critics accused him of doing
good in the name of the prince of evil. The answer is a very
simple one. If a man is doing something that is good, do not
accuse him of serving evil; it simply makes no sense. Inciden-
tally, preachers sometimes face this kind of criticism, and we
must make it clear that the accusation is against all logic. But
people such as those of the first century who were opponents of
the Lord are not open to logic. The comic strip character Pogo
has a word for us here: "We have met the enemy and he is us."

STAYING POWER

> "...but as it strikes no root in him he has no staying
> power, and when there is trouble or persecution on
> account of the word he falls away at once."   13:21

That phrase, "no staying power," expresses a main theme of
Jesus'. John Buchan said in his autobiography that fortitude is
the main virtue and that it means to keep on when you do not
feel like it. Then he added that the head man at that job was
the Apostle Paul. One of the main reasons why Paul was the
greatest Christian of all time and necessary to the Christian
church was his example of staying power. The good news is
that when a man surrenders himself to Jesus Christ and his
purposes, he receives that extra strength he must have in crucial
moments to stay.

The brilliant beginners are legion, but the men who will not quit are few. St. Paul writing to Timothy says: "The hour for my departure is upon me. I have run the great race, I have finished the course, I have kept the faith" (2 Timothy 4:6). For his summing of his life, he is saying, "I didn't quit." An adequate obituary!

MONEY'S FALSE GLAMOUR

"...but worldly cares and the false glamour of wealth choke it...."   13:22

The meaning of that phrase becomes clearer as we live. How many men would trade their wealth for a discovery of some meaning in life? What a good phrase is "the false glamour of wealth." What a pity it is that some of these truths come to us only with experience. There is nothing sentimental in this word of Jesus. A man once said, "I have been rich and I have been poor. Rich is better." Yes, there is no particular virtue in poverty. But to the man who has been blinded by the false glamour of money, there is only disappointment.

Our civilization has so yielded to this false glamour that advertising often makes possession of things the goal of all our striving. It reaches young minds as well as old. A seven-year-old noticed that although his mother dropped a bill into the offering basket, the lady next to her put in a small envelope. "She used her credit card," he confided to his mother.

Harry Golden said of an acquaintance who died suddenly, "My friend from Miami was successful and he boasted that he was rich. But I do not think he was really successful and I do not think he was really rich." Not if he allowed the good seeds to be choked.

THE NEW AND THE OLD

> "When, therefore, a teacher of the law has become a
> learner in the kingdom of Heaven, he is like a house-
> holder who can produce from his store both the new
> and the old." 13:52

When a man who is a teacher in the learned disciplines can become a learner in the kingdom of Heaven, he comes to a new point of view of the old and the new. It is difficult for a man to come to terms with these two common experiences. He may become so anxious for the new that he accepts it auto-matically, always assuming that it is bound to be better than the past. He may despise the old. On the other hand, he may become so enamored with yesterday that he never appreciates this morning's sunrise. How to live in a world and be at home both with the old and the new is the question.

We must come to terms with the truth that some things are neither old nor new but simply eternal. The past is a free univer-sity for us all and every man goes through it. If the past can relate to us in terms of the things that work and the things that are true, then all the past is to be remembered and its lessons passed along to the younger generation. To be unbound by it is the main thing; we need to regard it as a teacher guiding us into the future. The word that has helped me a great deal has been the closing part of Katherine Hankey's hymn "I Love To Tell the Story." She wrote:

> "And when, in scenes of glory,
> I sing the new, new song,
> 'Twill be the old, old story
> That I have loved so long."

So the gospel is always presenting us with the old, old story which has the quality of a new, new song.

THE HOME TOWN

> "A prophet will always be held in honour, except in
> his home town, and in his own family."   13:57

Distance lends enchantment. That with which we are familiar
seldom impresses us with greatness. It is the old story of no man
being great to his valet and no boy impressing the neighbors
with his talent. Most laymen regard their ministers as "men of
God," and even a proud fool may get away with this for a
considerable length of time if he is careful of his relationships
with his people. I never take the layman's remark about his
preacher as seriously as the word of one of his fellow preachers.
A man meets with his peers in all kind of conditions and situations where he is bound to reveal himself for what he is. So
when a preacher tells me that this man is real, I take it seriously.
Otherwise, I want to investigate for myself. But let us have
enough of these men who are experts far from home. For the
real and accurate estimate of a man, let us hear the word of the
hometown folks. If a man's character stands up to that test, you
can believe in him. That James, the brother of Jesus, became a
founder of the church is a great testimony to the daily nobility
and goodness of our Lord.

YOU FEED THEM

> "There is no need for them to go; give them some-
> thing to eat yourselves."   14:16

The church too often looks for someone else to help the people.
We depend upon the Community Chest to finance the few social
agencies which we operate. The hungry man is given a ticket
for the Salvation Army or the Mission. The preacher refers
those with nervous disturbances to a psychiatrist. We are like
the disciples whose advice was to send the people away to find

food. Jesus' command was, "Give them something to eat your-selves."

Perhaps it is time for us to reconsider the resources of the church and what we have in ourselves. We have something that is unique. We tend to treat symptoms, but the fundamental heal-ing for many a sick man is only to be found in what Jesus Christ can give him. We can give hope and faith.

DO NOT HESITATE

> "Why did you hesitate? How little faith you have!"
> 14:31

Peter started to walk across the water to meet Jesus. Suddenly, the story says, he was seized with fear, and that was his down-fall. What power there is in the man who never stops to think of all the things which might go wrong and all the powerful enemies who threaten. It is little faith that is our chief enemy. Unfortunately, there is often one such person on the governing board of a church. He is the man who weakens the church, not the power of the world. His negative view drives away courage.

I saw an exit from a parking lot with spikes pointing outward away from the exiting tires. A sign in large letters said, "Don't back up." A good Christian word!

TRADITION

> "You have made God's law null and void out of re-spect for your tradition."
> 15:7

Have you ever considered that too much respect for the secon-dary cancels out the primary thing in a man's life?

The main difference between God's law and man's tradition

is that the former is alive and the latter is dead. A contemporary theology has proclaimed that "God is dead," but the Bible was regarded by the Puritans as "the lively word of God." When we endeavor to change the lively word into a mere tradition, we have expressed our desire for something safe and our fear of life.

A banner unfurled in a Texas church read, "The seven last words of the church, 'We never did it that way before.'"

INSPIRATION

> Then Jesus said: "Simon son of Jonah, you are favoured indeed! You did not learn that from mortal man; it was revealed to you by my heavenly Father."
>
> 16:17

When a man gets an inspiration he takes the credit for it. This word of Jesus is a good one for the artist, writer, or preacher who suddenly has his eyes opened to some truth with deep spiritual implications. Where do these things come from? Anyone who has had the experience knows that it does not come from study or personal effort. Suddenly it is there, and if we are humble in spirit we will know that God put His favor upon us. Henry Ward Beecher, on being asked how he ever thought of the star illustration in one of his sermons, replied, "I saw it."

Andre Kostelanetz visited the painter Matisse at his Mediterranean home. "Where do you get your inspiration?" the musician asked the painter. "I grow artichokes," Matisse replied. "Every morning I go into the garden and watch these plants. I see the play of light and shade on the leaves and I discover new combination of colors and fantastic patterns. They inspire me. Then I go back to the studio and paint."

For the truths by which we live, we must wait patiently with Him until the moment they break upon our minds.

IT COSTS TOO MUCH

> "What will a man gain by winning the whole world,
> at the cost of his true self?" 16:26

Every man possesses a central core of integrity which is his real self. The world nibbles away at it until much of it disappears. Without it there is no criterion to differentiate the true from the false and there is no compass to set the direction a man's life ought to take. Having lost his true self, he is at the mercy of every liar, every pretender, and every hypocrite. As somebody said, the worst thing that happens to the liar is not that he can no longer believe anyone else, but that he can no longer believe himself.

The poet James Dickey writes, in *Self-Interview:* "The main thing that a teacher can do for a student is what Monroe Spears did for me, confirm the student in his desire to take literature seriously. This is important; in our technology-dominated world the value of literature is getting harder and harder to maintain, but it must be maintained if we're going to have any humanity left at all. The medical profession may save your life, but it can never make your life *worth* saving."

Listen to the words of Jawaharlal Nehru, in *Toward Freedom Day:* "The years I have spent in prison! Sitting alone, wrapped in my thoughts, how many seasons I have seen go by, following one another into oblivion! ... How many yesterdays of my youth lie buried here. Sometimes I see the ghosts of these dead yesterdays rise up and whisper to me, 'Was it worth-while?' There is no hesitation about the answer. ... My major decisions in public affairs would remain untouched. Indeed, I could not vary them, for they were stronger than myself, and a force beyond my control drove me to them."

35

FAITH UNLIMITED

"Your faith is too small." 17:20

The disciples could not heal the boy, and Jesus said, "Your faith is too small." This seems to have been the only measurement that Jesus put upon other people. His concern was not that they knew the right people, or had the right talents; just that they had a big enough faith. How many untalented, simple folks have done great works because their faith was large enough! How many people with great promise and many talents have been disappointments because they had faith in little other than themselves!

A big faith is necessary for a big work. If we have a job limited in its demands, then faith makes it shine with new possibilities.

We need faith in ourselves. A man always goes wrong if he thinks small about himself. We are saved from egotism by the larger faith that sees each man, including ourselves, as God's creation.

FOR CHILDREN ONLY

He called a child, set him in front of them, and said, "I tell you this: unless you turn round and become like children, you will never enter the kingdom of Heaven." 18:2-3

Sartre said: "We're not put on this earth to be demi-gods, but only to improve a little." Jesus says: "Become like children."

Children are not so proud that they must stay the same way to save their pride. They can "turn round" when it becomes apparent they are on the wrong way. Our Lord implies that repentance and becoming like children go together.

Nor should we assume that "the kingdom of Heaven" is not

an attractive state for children. A black Baptist church was holding its worship service on a Sunday morning in Milwaukee. The windows and doors were open, for it was a summer day. As a family went by on the way to another church, their seven-year-old asked his mother, "Why can't we go to this church? They have a lot more fun than we do."

Consider what the kingdom of Heaven is like if we must become like children in order to enter it.

OFF THE RECORD

> **"If your brother commits a sin, go and take the matter up with him, strictly between yourselves, and if he listens to you, you have won your brother over."**
> 18:15

It is the custom of some preachers to drive people into a corner. They seem to be bent on making their opponents confess that they have been altogether wrong and publicly deny their positions. It is the part of wisdom to let a man find an easy way out if he has been convinced that he is wrong. There are instances which will come to every pastor when he and another should speak "strictly between yourselves." If the other person listens, we have won a brother. If he will not listen, there are still some things we may do. Let us not forget that six important words in the language are: "I admit I made a mistake." They are also the most difficult to say. A preacher ought to make their saying as easy as possible.

WHERE IS HE?

> "For where two or three have met together in my
> name, I am there among them."   18:20

In all discussion of whether God is to be found "out there" or
"up there" or within us, here is a clear word about where we are
to find Christ. He is standing with the people who meet together
in His name.

The idea that religion can be found only when we are alone
does not find support in the New Testament. In the eighteenth
century John Wesley emphasized that the only holiness the
Bible knows anything about is social holiness. There may be
some religions which find their high point in withdrawing from
human contact, but it is not true of Christianity.

Where shall we find Christ? In action. In the struggle. In
the concern we share for a better life for our brethren.

Where do we feel closest to him? When we are with our
brethren waging a brave fight for men. Alfred North White-
head wrote, in *Adventures of Ideas* (Macmillan, 1933): "In an
age of aristocracy in England, the Methodists appealed to the
direct intuition of working men and of retail traders concerned
with working men. In America they appealed to the toiling
isolated groups of pioneers. They brought hope, fear, emotional
release, spiritual insight. They stemmed the inroads of revolutionary ideas. Also, allowing for many qualifications, they must
be credited with one supreme achievement. They made the
brotherhood of man and the importance of men a vivid reality.
They had produced the final effective force which hereafter
made slavery impossible among progressive races."

We find Him in fellowship with those who undertake a
brave purpose in His name.

YOU SCOUNDREL

> " 'You scoundrel!' he said to him; 'I remitted the
> whole of your debt when you appealed to me; were
> you not bound to show your fellow-servant the same
> pity as I showed you?' "   18:33

"Scoundrel" is the word needed here, and it is followed by a
sharp expression: "were you not bound to show your fellow-
servant the same pity as I showed you?" The forgiveness of our
Lord throws a terrible responsibility on us. It binds us to forgive
those who sin against us and it demands that we be as forgiving
to our brethren as Christ has been to us. It is a terrifying thing
to be forgiven.

Early in the nineteenth century, a man named George Wilson
killed a government employee who had caught him robbing the
mail. He was tried and sentenced to hang. However, President
Andrew Jackson sent him a pardon. But Wilson for some unknown reason refused to accept it and no one knew what to do.
The case went to the United States Supreme Court. Chief Justice
Marshall wrote the decision: "A pardon is a slip of paper, the
value of which is determined by the acceptance of the person to
be pardoned. If it is refused, it is no pardon. George Wilson
must be hanged." And he was.

The acceptance of God's pardon does not become valid until
it is accepted and shared.

GO THE WHOLE WAY

> Jesus said to him, "If you wish to go the whole way,
> go, sell your possessions...."   19:21

No man ought to begin the Christian life unless he intends to
go the whole way. Some things in life ought to be settled, and
our commitment to One we shall call Lord ought to be one of
the things we settle permanently.

This is a word about happiness. To be happy we must go in one direction toward a goal with all our might. It engrosses all our energy. The sinner is unhappy because he is haunted by something he ought to be, and the saint is unhappy if he wants to do something which is forbidden. But the man who is willing to "go the whole way" finds a great and divine surprise waiting for him. As C. S. Lewis expressed it in his autobiography, he is "Surprised by Joy."

JEALOUS OF KINDNESS

"Why be jealous because I am kind?"   20:15

At the beginning of the story Jesus says that those who had started to work early in the morning "expected something extra" beyond what those who came into the fields late received. But when they objected that they deserved more than those who had not worked so long, Jesus' reply was that men should not be jealous of the kindness of God. There is a basic justice in God's rule and then there is the extra kindness and the grace which He bestows upon men.

The human inclination is to resent anyone else having what we cannot enjoy ourselves. I talked with a man recently who was bitter over what he called the easy time young people have today compared with the hard time he had experienced in his youth. The longer he talked the more he sounded like the complaining laborers in the parable.

ON GIVING ORDERS

> "I want you," she said, "to give orders that in your
> kingdom my two sons here may sit next to you, one
> at your right, and the other at your left."   20:21

Have you ever considered how seldom Jesus gave orders? The
one who took unto himself the form of a servant and said that
his followers must be as servants, was not in the habit of order-
ing people around. Yet we must remember that he spoke as one
who had authority. Dictatorship is a form of government which
always appears powerful until the end. Or consider how the
dictatorial father has his way until suddenly there is a rebellion
and the youth walks out. Every pastor has such examples in his
own counseling experience. But consider the plight of the
authoritarian church when the people have had enough of it.
We ought not to forget the limitations of giving orders.

TIME TO SHOUT

> When they heard it said that Jesus was passing they
> shouted, "Have pity on us, Son of David." The
> people told them sharply to be quiet. But they
> shouted all the more....   20:30-31

There was an old Scotch preacher who in the middle of a prayer
said, "And thou knowest, O Lord, that I am not in the habit of
being denied." Not always, but sometimes, men storm the gates
of Heaven and cry out with such insistence that they are heard.
There is power in sheer persistence.

F. Olin Stockwell, writing about his prison experiences in
Red China, said, "The fact that the New Testament was written
by people who were themselves suffering and *for* people who
were in difficulty, makes it understandable only to those who
have a real feeling of need. If life is pleasant for you and you

have no hungers you cannot satisfy, you do not need to read the New Testament. For you will not know what it is talking about. But when the winds of ill-fortune begin to blow or when the hand of fate takes you by the scuff of the neck and puts you behind the locked doors of economic collapse, moral failure, sickness, or death, open your New Testament. You will find out what it means then" *(With God in Red China)*.

CONGREGATION WILD WITH EXCITEMENT

> When he entered Jerusalem the whole city went wild
> with excitement.   21:10

Connected with every great evangelical revival there has been excitement. When was the last time anybody got excited in your church or mine? Too often we are more concerned that everything remain quiet and that our people have peace of mind. The presence of Jesus sometimes brings quiet and calm, but more often it brings a kind of uproar. Monsignor Knox closed his study of religious movements entitled *Enthusiasm* with a quotation from Edmund Rostand's *La Princesse lointaine*. Brother Trophine said that inertia is the only vice, and answered the question: what is the only virtue, with one word: "Enthusiasm." Beset by the dangers of excess as it is, nothing is done without this power of enthusiasm.

BOYS SHOUTING IN THE TEMPLE

> The chief priests and doctors of the law saw the wonderful things he did, and heard the boys in the temple shouting, "Hosanna to the Son of David," and they asked him indignantly, "Do you hear what they are saying?" Jesus answered, "I do; have you never read that text, 'Thou hast made children and babes at the breast sound aloud thy praise'?"
>
> 21:15-16

The place of children in the church is always debatable for some people. We ought to remember that now and again children see things plainer than adults. Young people's criticisms of society should be heard. We know they have not had the experience adults have had, but they see more clearly the way things ought to be. They are unencumbered with regulations and rules of the past. Children are our hope of growth and progress. If they have an eye for what is wrong, they know when greatness appears.

Dick Van Dyke, in *Faith, Hope and Hilarity* (Doubleday, 1970), tells about a pastor in Riverside, California, dressed in clerical garb, who was visiting a class of four-year-olds to explain his job to them. The teacher said to them, "Children, we have a special guest this morning, do you know who he is?" One little boy asked tentatively, "God?" "No," said the teacher, "but he works for God." Then the pastor proceeded to tell the class about his work as spiritual leader of the church. As he started to leave, the same little boy said, "Next time, bring God with you. I've never seen him." But when the children saw Jesus, they thought they had seen God.

THE RIGHT WAY

> "For when John came to show you the right way to
> live, you did not believe him, but the tax-gatherers
> and prostitutes did...." 21:32

It is hard for people to believe that Christianity tells us "the
right way to live." It is not just a way to save our souls nor a
way to prepare our spirits for heaven. The gospel is the revelation of the way things are, and it gives us guidelines for survival.
Even tax collectors and prostitutes, when it seems too late for
them, recognize that this is the way life should be lived. Then
when they accept it, they are given new chances. It is the
righteous, the smugly satisfied, who cannot see through their
own so-called "religious" procedures to the simple truth of what
the gospel is.

I had a friend who became an alcoholic and finally was cured.
He went back to church, which he had neglected, and his family
all became active again. He wrote me a long letter one day, the
main point being that the pastor of his church called on his
family the night before. Now this man's father had been a
minister, and he knew that pastoral calls were not something
unusual. But suddenly it all looked new and different after what
he had been through and the simple fact of a visit seemed a
wonderful thing in his eyes. Sometimes it is only the experience
of being lost which opens our minds to His authority.

THE HONOUR OF HIS INVITATION

> " '...but the guests I invited did not deserve the
> honour.' " 22:8

Accepting God's invitation in the gospel is not granting God a
favor. God's gracious invitation is an honor that has been bestowed upon us. The repentant sinner never gets over marveling

at the harm he did which God in His mercy overlooked with an invitation to attend his feast. Jesus' teaching is not servility nor is his humility apologetic. His great word is of an honor extended to all. When we see it, we accept with joyful humility.

We need a new attitude toward the church. I never felt it incumbent upon me to give announcements of other organizations in the church service. One of Dr. Harry Emerson Fosdick's most appreciated characteristics was an unwillingness to travel around the country making speeches. He was the minister of the Riverside Church and if they wanted to hear him in person, that is where they were invited to be present. The church came first, and nothing could be compared with the honor of being ordained to offer its invitation every Sunday in the church.

TAKEN BY SURPRISE

This answer took them by surprise....   22:22

Corita Kent, a former Catholic nun who draws with inspiration, said, "To believe in God is to know that all the rules are fair and that there will be wonderful surprises." A recent book by a sociologist described the ability of his discipline to foretell what was going to happen in the future. He said the purpose of the process was to give us a "surpriseless" world. This is a great difference between religion and the social disciplines. The man who follows Christ will have surprises at every turn, and wonder will come to him in the most prosaic circumstances. A world that loses its sense of God loses its ability to be surprised. This generation needs nothing more than the presence of the One who is always taking us by surprise.

A great prayer contains this striking sentence: "If we have come into the service of worship thinking to leave just as we came, visit us with a divine surprise." God is always surprising us if we will allow Him, and the church needs surprise. We have been covered with too many layers of safe, dull orthodoxy. If the preacher can now and then surprise his congregation by what he says or the way he says it, he serves the kingdom of God.

ROAD BLOCKS

> "You shut the door of the kingdom of Heaven in men's faces; you do not enter yourselves, and when others are entering, you stop them."   23:13

This unlovely quality is not confined just to lawyers and Pharisees. It is the attitude which says that if I cannot have it nobody else will have it. It is a jealousy that arises when another person has an experience which you did not care enough about to claim for yourself. We do not intend to go that way ourselves, and we will make it difficult for those who do.

A politician may not intend to do anything about a need personally, but he does not want his opponent to get credit for doing it either. The legalist does not intend to help, but he opposes anyone else's attempt to help. It is a mean, narrow, jealous spirit that enters into some marriages. This husband is not happy, so he sees to it that neither his wife nor his children know any happiness.

The Christian is one who opens doors for other people and finds his joy when they enter the new experience of the kingdom. St. Paul described the quality when he said that love is never boastful, nor conceited, nor rude; never selfish, not quick to take offense (1 Corinthians 13:4-5). It is, as Henry Drummond called it, "the greatest thing in the world."

APPEARANCES ARE DECEIVING

> "...outside you look like honest men, but inside you
> are brim-full of hypocrisy and crime."   23:28

The Bible in the language of another day sounds quaint; we lose the sense of its direct, hard attack. Preachers sometimes think they are speaking hard truth to the people, but because they use academic language the point never quite comes through. Jesus' words were hard, and his attack on the Pharisees and their hypocrisy came with the force of whips. One begins to understand why they were so angry and why they plotted his destruction. Those who are forever counseling gentle speech will find no comfort in this translation of his hard words.

A man was given the nickname of "Honest Joe." It embarrassed him and he protested he did not deserve it. "Couldn't you call me 'Fairly Honest Joe?' " he asked. The word of Jesus was more severe than just tempering the title a bit. "You look honest but you are not," was his judgment.

BIRTH PANGS OF A NEW AGE

> "For nation will make war upon nation, kingdom
> upon kingdom; there will be famines and earth-
> quakes in many places. With all these things the
> birth-pangs of the new age begin."   24:7-8

A scientist at the University of California wrote that the golden age is always at the end of a period and never the sign of a beginning. The so-called golden age is really a sign of deterioration and death. Beginnings mean birth pangs. Jesus describes the beginnings of the new age as a time of war, of famine and earthquake. The future is often born in an explosion.

Think of our day in the light of this verse. We are aware of the civil rights revolution, the feminine revolution, and the wars abroad. Not many people think this is very hopeful, and you can read few descriptions of the contemporary world without concluding that we live in a very bad time. But according to this scriptural insight, these disturbances are the birth pains of something new and wonderful.

When Wordsworth wrote:

> Bliss was it in that dawn to be alive,
> But to be young was very heaven!

he was talking about the French Revolution. One theory of the creation of the earth is that it began with an explosion that broke off this little planet from a much larger mass. Think about explosions as the God of creativity at work.

KEEP AWAKE!

> "Keep awake, then; for you do not know on what day your Lord is to come." 24:42

This ought to take care of all those who set a particular date for the Second Coming and the end of the world. His word is "Keep awake."

I thought as I drove home the other night on the freeway that most accidents take place when people are careless and not alert. The constant prayer of a man driving a car ought to be, "Keep me awake."

Life goes wrong when drowsiness dulls our moral sense. The man who finds his life in ruins is hard put to tell just when or how it happened. Let us not be lulled into a torpor by our carelessness.

What a good word this is for the church in its worship. The trouble, brethren, is simply that our services are dull and so is our preaching.

Christians, and all who follow in His train, impress those

they meet because they are alive. How much we miss by being
half-asleep. Keep awake!

THINK SMALL

> " 'You have proved trustworthy in a small way; I will
> now put you in charge of something big."   25:21

It is a common human weakness to have no enthusiasm for the
small thing and to expect something big immediately. I was
playing golf with a friend of mine some years ago, and asked
him about his younger son, who was about ready to graduate
from college. "What is Joe going to do?" I asked. His father
replied, "Oh, he doesn't know, but he is willing to start anywhere just so it's at the top." The church polity which assumes
that every young man needs to start with a small group and
work gradually to the larger church is looked upon suspiciously
by young men with ability and ambition. They find it hard to
believe that they need experience in small things.

The events that influence our lives most are unnoticeable
when they happen. It is a word of encouragement or a simple
act of courtesy or a small cry for help that shapes our futures.
It is doing unto the least of the brethren as if they were Christ
himself that marks God's judgment.

The Volkswagen motor company had a sign some time ago,
"Think Small." It is a good word for Christians. For it turns out
that what some people overlook as inconsequential represents
the issue containing all the importance of eternity. In the
stimulating book, *The Peter Principle,* it is said: "In a hierarchy
every employee tends to rise to his level of incompetence." For
institutions, this is the judgment.

HUMBLE MEN AND KINGS

> "And the king will answer, 'I tell you this: anything
> you did for one of my brothers here, however hum-
> ble, you did for me.' " 25:40

Horace Bushnell said that the gospel is a gift to the imagination.
There is no place where this is clearer than at the end of the
parable of the judgment. We do not have enough imagination
to grasp the truth of this word, so we distribute our goodness
according to the status of the recipients. Jesus identifies himself
with the humblest brethren. We are discovering that these
humble brethren are as important as kings. It is their hunger
and their hurt that defines the future of nations and societies.
It is the black revolt that brings democracy to its greatest and
final test. And so it turns out again that what sounded to us as
idealistic and sentimental, proves to be simply a revelation of
the way things are. We must learn or be destroyed.

YOU MEAN ME?

> In great distress they exclaimed one after the other,
> "Can you mean me, Lord?" 26:22

Jesus confounded the disciples with his accusation, and they
were startled that he had one of them in mind. When I read the
gospels in this version, I am impressed anew with the directness
of Jesus' word and the impossibility of escaping his searching
examinations.

Americans sometimes assume that everything their country
does is beyond question and beyond criticism. It comes as a
real shock to an American citizen to listen to the interpretation
put upon some of our actions in foreign countries. We have
been the society which upsets family life in Japan. Our financial
manipulations bring distress to people we have never seen. We

are looked upon as warmongers, and not as defenders of democracy. An American wants to cry out in rebellion and ask, "Can you mean me"?

The church always needs this direct word. A churchman who has grown up within the fellowship of the church cannot believe the harsh word spoken by the atheist or the secularist. We discover that all along we have been judging the church in terms of its intentions, and not its actual accomplishments. Those on the outside pay little attention to our high-sounding purpose. They look simply at the meager accomplishment. The churchman needs to hear their word, and ask, "Can you mean me?"

I need this experience and so do you. I may be sure that a personal criticism is unfair and unjust and arises out of either prejudice or ignorance. But when I try to defend myself, my case does not sound convincing even to me. It is a sure sign of a mature Christian when he can hear his Lord's word about betrayal and instead of defending himself begins to look with fresh eyes upon himself and his actions.

SIT WITH ME

"Stop here, and stay awake with me."   26:39

This was a time when Jesus needed friends to help him. They could not take away the cup he had to drink, but how much it would have helped if they stayed awake and shared his grief.

This is the pastor's role. A man gets upset because he does not know the answers to hard questions. How useless we feel when a man cries out in the agony of his soul for an answer to one of those unanswerable questions. But let the pastor not despair. Sometimes to just be there for awhile as a friend means much to the sufferer. The old lady who called on her friend whose husband had just died was asked by a neighbor what she said at a time like that. The old lady replied, "I did not say anything. I just made her a cup of tea." Do not play it down when that is all you can do. For any man who has walked through the valley of pain or defeat knows how much it means just to have somebody with him. What a sad thing it was that the disciples had an opportunity to minister unto the Lord and fell asleep.

I AM GUILTY

> "I have sinned," he said; "I have brought an innocent
> man to his death." 27:4

Judas regrets the whole business when he comes to himself, but that is of no concern to those who bribed him for his betrayal. His trouble now is with himself.

In John Masefield's "Everlasting Mercy" the repentant sinner, Saul Kane, speaks of the harm he had done by being himself. This is the final punishment of the sinner and it is felt by every man. Judas is not some extraordinary villain. Judas is me. There is no protection from self-accusation, and the psychologist can give us plenty of examples of men who never are able to cope with guilt and are destroyed by it. A great thing about the gospel is the forgiving answer in Christ.

The Christian's prayer always resembles John Newton's words when he heard that a neighboring curate had been burned to death in a fire he had started "being in liquor." Newton wrote: "Lord, may I remember thy patience toward me when I drank down iniquity. Why was I not surprised in my sins and hurried to judgment!"

SILENCE

> ...but he still refused to answer one word, to the
> Governor's great astonishment.   27:14

The governor expected alibis, but he did not know how to deal
with silence. Accused men always insist that they have been
accused unjustly. A king visiting his prison listened to the im-
passioned words of innocence and false arrest by every prisoner
except one, who confessed he was guilty. "Let this man go free,"
commanded the king. "I do not want all these innocent men
to be contaminated by the presence of one guilty man." Preachers
are excuse-making creatures. No preacher is ever to blame for
anything, and he can always find people to blame if things go
wrong. There is the official board of the church, or there is the
Women's Society, or there is jealousy on the part of a colleague.
But a man who just keeps silent and accepts the situation
without explanation is truly impressive. You wonder what kind
of a man he is and what is back of his quiet dignity.

Great men do this, while lesser men are never quite up to it.
General Lee, after the disastrous charge at Gettysburg, rode
among his men saying it was his fault completely and they must
simply rally to what they had left and save what they could.
Imagine a man in a situation like that trying to explain the
disaster.

WHICH JESUS DO YOU WANT?

> "Which would you like me to release to you—Jesus
> Bar-Abbas, or Jesus called Messiah?"   27:17

It is a little shocking to realize that the man they released instead
of Jesus Christ also had the first name of Jesus. The New English
Bible takes the testimony of some of the ancient manuscripts
and, besides heightening the drama of the scene, makes us

understand that Jesus was a common name. We discover that today, in countries south of the border, it is not at all unusual for men to have the name Jesus. But for us two thousand years have made that name apply only to one person. What's in a name, indeed! The name now is filled with the gospel story of our Lord who came and died and rose again. It is man's authority to put names on objects and, as Shakespeare says, to give things "a local habitation and a name." Christian revelation tells us that this is what God has done in Jesus. That which was general and obscure and hard to understand is now given a name. Or, as one writer put it, religion has become biography.

THE WORD!

> "He has been raised from the dead and is going on before you into Galilee; there you will see him." That is what I had to tell you.   28:7

How direct and simple this is. He was dead; he was raised from the dead; and he goes on before you. That is the message in a nutshell. That is the gospel story in brief. Every sermon can be brought under the searching light of this word and judged. He was dead; he is alive; he goes before us.

BE ASSURED

> "And be assured..."   28:20

The last word of the good news in Matthew is assurance. After all has been said and done, we can say "and be assured." We must not be guilty of "cheap" assurance. Our word is of the best which begins with the worst.

Mrs. Joseph Fairchild Knapp, wife of the founder of the

Metropolitan Life Insurance Company, was a hymn writer. One day she took a tune to Fanny Crosby and asked, "What does this tune say to you?" After a few minutes of thought the reply came, "Blessed assurance, Jesus is mine." That well-known hymn, sung by so many Christians, was the result.

There is something about the story of Jesus that acts on the hearts of men as Mrs. Knapp's tune acted on Fanny Crosby. It says to us: Be assured. The Christian is not one who escapes, but one who has been assured.

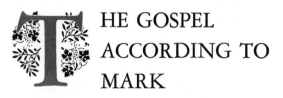

THE GOSPEL ACCORDING TO MARK

INTRODUCTION

> Jesus said to them, "Come with me, and I will make
> you fishers of men." And at once they left their nets
> and followed him. 1:17

The Gospels are word portraits of our Lord. They are not photo-
graphs, of course, any more than they are academic, scholarly
biographies. They are pictures of Jesus from men who were
committed to him. Mark is probably the earliest, written somewhere between A.D. 65 and 70. Mark's mother was one of the
church hostesses of those early days, and a Christian church met
in her home. She was apparently a well-to-do widow and there-
fore had a larger house then most of her neighbors. So Mark
grew up in the atmosphere of the early church.

He went on the first missionary journey with Paul and Barnabas, but he left them and came home before they had finished
the journey. We do not know the reason: it may have been that
he had a girl back home, or maybe he was homesick. Mark's
action made Paul angry, and when a second journey was planned
he refused to take Mark along. An argument with Barnabas,
who was Mark's cousin, became so bitter that Paul and Barnabas
separated and on the second journey Paul took Silas with him.
It is good news that later Paul regarded Mark as his friend and
Christian brother. In the Second Letter to Timothy, Paul requested that Mark be brought to him at Rome. "Pick up Mark
and bring him with you," Paul wrote, "for I find him a useful
assistant" (2 Timothy 4:11).

Pappias, one of the early bishops, in A.D. 140 wrote the famous passage in which he said that Mark was Peter's interpreter and that he wrote down what Peter remembered about Jesus, although not in order. The gospel sounds like Peter from what we know of his temperament and spirit. It reflects a great interest in what Jesus did and the mighty acts of God carried out through him.

In this gospel primarily we see a God who acts. This is no leisurely description of the attributes of a Deity. He is not the aristocratic gentleman of the universe; as William James pointed out long ago, if you are looking for a gentleman, you will find him in the Prince of Darkness. God does too many menial things with which no gentleman would be involved. He is not Aristotle's "unmoved mover," nor is he the celestial chess player of T. H. Huxley, making every move perfectly without either approbation or resentment and dispassionately checkmating our poor efforts when we make blunders.

The God of this gospel is involved in the human situation, and he is the God of history. Instead of finding history an embarrassment and something to escape, Christianity takes it seriously. I heard a lecturer say a shocking thing: God is a celestial garbage collector. Man finds himself sitting on a garbage heap with its stench in his nostrils, and it is only God's removal of the garbage that makes life livable and the atmosphere breathable. He is the God of action.

We have here a sharp insight into the nature of man. An age of revolution will find much in this gospel to fit its mood. If, as a brilliant scholar once said, "All revolution is a revolt against authority," we can understand that point of view. It is truer to say, however, that revolution is usually a revolt against neglect. The black revolution and the student revolution are demands for more involvement in the administration of American society and its decisions. Revolutions are another witness to the demand of all men for action.

The Gospel of Mark calls us to danger. It puts its emphasis on what Jesus did more than what he said. Two American students in Germany, having learned the German language well enough to understand lectures, went to hear a famous German philosopher. After listening for ten minutes, one of them turned to the other and said. "This is very dull. Let us leave." But his friend replied, "Well, I admit it is dull, but let us at least wait until he gets to the verb." The Gospel of Mark likes the verbs of the Christian faith.

GET READY!

> In the prophet Isaiah it stands written: "Here is my herald whom I send on ahead of you, and he will prepare your way. A voice crying aloud in the wilderness, 'Prepare a way for the Lord; clear a straight path for him.' "   1:2-3

Immediately we are plunged into the story. Jesus Christ is the one Isaiah described. His task is to prepare the way for God, and it is Jesus' cousin John who is the forerunner for his ministry and the voice crying in the wilderness. One has the sense right at the beginning that something tremendous is going to take place. It is a word of high expectancy and it ought to guide us as ministers when we begin a service of worship. We are not to set a mood of cold and aloof contemplation. This is the place to claim the promises of God and our hearts must be filled with anticipation. For our own preaching it would be well to remember that we are not to meander around at the beginning as if we had all day. Get to the heart of it immediately, for there is no time to waste. Great preaching plunges us immediately into the atmosphere of action. A visitor to the Grand Canyon looked at that mighty panorama and said, "Man, something happened here." That is what men say when they read the Gospel of Mark.

AUTHORITY

> They were all dumbfounded and began to ask one
> another, "What is this? A new kind of teaching! He
> speaks with authority. When he gives orders, even
> the unclean spirits submit."   1:27

One can feel the crackling spirit of excitement in these words.
There was nothing dull in it, and when Jesus spoke they listened
as if he gave orders and had a right to do so.

What the New English Bible has done for the scriptures, the
preacher must do for his congregation. His must be the testimony
of a man who bears witness to what he has discovered and experienced. He has the authority within himself.

For us, authority grows out of complete dedication to Jesus
Christ. Talented men have always known that their gifts were
never a release from hard work. Bach used to say to his students:
"I had to work hard. Whoever works as hard as I did, will get
just as far." One of his biographers, Forkel, tells us, "His inborn
talent he evidently counted worth nothing." Goethe wrote some
lines which may be translated: "Natural gifts—who wouldn't
have them? Talents? Children's toys! To be earnest, makes the
man; to work hard, the genius."

Good words for Christians!

THE WHOLE TOWN WAS THERE

> ...and the whole town was there, gathered at the
> door.   1:33

Right at the beginning of Jesus' ministry he was surrounded by
crowds. They brought all their sick to be healed, and any who
were in any kind of difficulty tried to get his attention. Remember
that when the soldiers were sent to seize him before the crucifixion, he said it was not necessary to arrest him secretly and at

night. He had been before them doing his work openly all the time.

Lord Acton said, "Everything secret degenerates: nothing is safe that does not show it can bear discussion and publicity." Jesus and the church have stood in the blinding light of publicity for two thousand years. The scholars have looked at the scriptures and weighed their claims on the scales of probability. They have searched every source possible to find contradictions and contrary evidence. Here right at the beginning of his ministry Jesus found himself under the searching eyes of the crowd.

Weigh this against the procedures of secret organizations. These exclusive groups hide their memberships and reveal their ritual only to the initiates. They are the modern "mystery religions." The Christian church, to a great extent under the influence of the Protestant Reformation, has not taken refuge in secret formulas or passwords but has borne its witness openly and without guile.

MOVE OUT

> He answered, "Let us move on to the country towns in the neighbourhood; I have to proclaim my message there also; that is what I came out to do."   1:38

Jesus considered it his calling first of all to proclaim the good news. How easily he could have become a healer or a miracle worker! But his faith was in the proclamation, and whether it was Jerusalem or the country towns, this was his primary responsibility. Preaching is not just one activity among many, it is the foundation upon which the whole of the church is built.

62

SOMETHING MORE BESIDES

> He also said, "Take note of what you hear; the measure you give is the measure you will receive, with something more besides." 4:24

It is that "something more besides" that is impossible to define. If we are under law, we make a bargain and expect the exact return that is promised. Since we are under grace, the whole agreement goes far beyond what we expect or what we have any right to ask. It is these "golden extras" which make the Christian life so full of joy.

A happy marriage is never definable, because there are those things in it which are something more. The Christian home has so many experiences which no man can set down on paper. Whenever a man does his duty and fulfills his obligation, something is added to the whole experience which he never counted on and never asked for.

This is true of the whole Christian experience; we always feel that half has never been told. G. K. Chesterton, speaking of the Franciscan friars, said they were perpetually coming and going on all the highways and byways of Italy seeking to ensure that any man who met one of them by chance should have a spiritual adventure. Christians always have "something more besides" to share.

ARE WE ABLE?

> With many such parables he would give them his message, so far as they were able to receive it. 4:33

It is a rule of life that a man only hears what he is able to hear. Many times as we grow older a thing becomes perfectly clear which when we first heard it made very little sense to us. In the meantime, we have had some experiences and gone through some situations which prepared our minds for his truth. An English Prime Minister suffering from gout once remarked, "If I had known these legs were going to carry a Prime Minister, I would have taken better care of them when I was young." It is the source of despair to the teacher or to the father that what he knows is true cannot be made clear to the young because they are not "able to receive it." The truth of God's revelation can only be revealed when a man is able to perceive it.

The prophets were men who could see God's will and God's plan in ordinary things. So the older man ought to be a better preacher than the younger man. He has had more things happen to him which open his eyes to God's hidden writing. Experience makes the blank page come alive with God's wisdom. Every parent and every teacher knows this experience.

GO HOME

> Jesus would not allow it, but said to him, "Go home to your own folk and tell them what the Lord in his mercy has done for you."   5:19

We prefer doing our religious work far from home, and we respond to cries for help from overseas. Jesus told this man that he had to begin where he was; the need was not for another traveling companion but for a witness at home. That was a hard command.

A church may be generous to a missionary enterprise in Africa but deaf to a cry for help next door. The young preacher must go somewhere in the deep South to make his witness, while a riot is getting ready to happen in Watts or Detroit or Harlem. I have known laymen who were almost professionals in visiting churches and talking about tithing. When I inquired about them in their home church, nobody knew anything about their giving or their Christian service. I had a man like that in my own Conference. I never could find a single instance of his generosity in his own community. The best place to be a Christian is right where you are now.

WHERE DOES HE GET IT?

> ...and the large congregation who heard were amazed and said, "Where does he get it from? ..."
> 6:2

They did not assume that Jesus had been reading a new book. That is where much of our own information comes from, and much of our teaching. They did not ask what school he had attended or who had been teaching him. They knew they had heard an original who could never be explained by ordinary means.

In the crucial moments of a nation's life, where does its strength come from? Not from the contemporary scene, but from a great source, half-forgotten and ignored. Where does a man get the power and the courage for the great moment in his own life? It comes out of his belief and his faith. The man who helps the people when he speaks is a man who knows God personally. And when we find such a one, we know what Einstein meant when he said: "The most beautiful thing we can experience is the mysterious. It is the source of all true art and science. He to whom this emotion is a stranger, who can no longer pause to wonder and stand in awe, is as good as dead; his eyes are closed." The Incarnation is always a mystery and always a miracle.

QUIET!

He said to them, "Come with me, by yourselves, to some lonely place where you can rest quietly." 6:31

In a day of many organizations and much activity, it is difficult to hear these words without being troubled in our conscience. When was the last time we drew apart to a lonely place where we could rest quietly? The Gospel of Mark talks about action, but it will not let us forget times when Jesus took his disciples apart to rest and to be restored. One of the worst pollutions of our time is noise. Said Pascal: "All the mischief in the world is done by one thing: the inability to remain at rest within one's own room." The man whose life is given to business and economic affairs which he must tend to, and then turns Sunday into just another day of travel and noise, begins to run down. When I consider the way most people live, I am not surprised that one of our most common diseases is mental illness. If we are to work hard and be productive, let us find those lonely places where we can rest quietly.

Paul Mellon is an unusual kind of man and, among other things, an unpublicized conservationist. He once said. "What we often really need is an hour alone, to dream, to contemplate or simply to feel the sun. What this country needs is a good five-cent reverie."

DULLNESS WITHIN AND WITHOUT

He said to them, "Are you as dull as the rest?"
7:18

It is a word to Christians and church members. We are not surprised when the world fails to comprehend the demands of the gospel and the meaning of its message. But what shall we say when the church, instead of bearing a clear witness, shows

the same confusions within its fellowship that are found outside of it? The church, as you recall, has been compared with
Noah's Ark: only the raging of the storm outside enables the
passengers to put up with the stench within. The preacher finds
it difficult to have patience with all the pettiness and blindness
he encounters among his own flock. Jesus had to bear with
this kind of response among his own disciples. It is dullness that
causes our betrayal and our failure to understand. John Wesley
was much impressed with some of the electrical treatments in
his day and he thought they would benefit the health of his
people. "Be electrified daily," was his advice, and it is also the
spirit of Jesus.

NO HIDING PLACE

> He found a house to stay in, and he would have liked
> to remain unrecognized, but this was impossible.
>
> 7:24

People who prefer to be unrecognized are rare, and an inordinate
seeking of publicity is one of the more unlovely characteristics
of this generation. I live in a part of the world that is notorious
for publicity tricks to attract notice. But there is also another
side to this, and the Christian, especially the preacher, oftentimes desires quiet with no recognition. But this, too, is impossible, for when a man becomes a Christian he is on display.
People find us out in spite of ourselves and regard us as examples of this faith. A friend of mine from the east joined me
for lunch in downtown Los Angeles. When I asked him what
he had been doing that morning, he said, "I have been walking
around the city and I'm disillusioned. Coming by a large church
with a large sign *Church of the Open Door,* I found it locked
up tight."

Once we accept Christ publicly we have shut the door on the

privilege of being "unrecognized." Those who are broken-hearted and lost will be sure to seek us out if they find that we have been with Him. Recognition, instead of being something to seek, is for the Christian an occupational hazard of his profession.

GET LOST!

> "Whoever cares for his own safety is lost; but if a man will let himself be lost for my sake and for the Gospel, that man is safe."   8:35

Should a man ever let himself get lost? Should not a Christian always know where he is and where he is going? But the text brought to my mind a phrase of Charles Wesley's hymn, "Love Divine, All Loves Excelling." In the fourth stanza he wrote:

> Till we cast our crowns before Thee,
> Lost in wonder, love and praise.

That is the place where a Christian gets lost—in his Christian experience. Jesus is speaking of being freed from concern for safety and losing oneself in the grandeur and wonder of Jesus Christ and his good news. Is there not in every man who has been captured by a vision or a deep spiritual experience a kind of "lostness"? Something has happened to him that is beyond his comprehension and beyond his analysis. St. Paul had experienced it. He wrote: "For I reckon that the sufferings we now endure bear no comparison with the splendour, as yet unrevealed, which is in store for us" (Romans 8:18). Every now and again the Apostle was lost as he thought of the gifts which had been given to him by Christ and the future which awaited him in the heavenly kingdom.

WHAT PRICE CHARACTER?

"What can he give to buy that self back?" 8:37

Some things are not reversible. If you have sold your life to the world and now you want it back, what price can you give? The whole matter is settled and final with no possibility of buying back what you have so carelessly bargained away. The good news of the gospel comes to say that the mercy of God and the love of Christ will give us another chance. Our true selves are beyond all price and all bargaining and they are the treasures to be kept at all costs. Dick Shepherd thought the question he would have to answer at the Last Judgment was: "Well, what did you make of it?"

DON'T ARGUE!

> When they came back to the disciples they saw a large crowd surrounding them and lawyers arguing with them. 9:14

A man whose boy was sick was there, and the lawyers were arguing. Jesus asked what the argument was about. Of one thing we can be sure, they did not see the need of this father and the sickness of the boy. Instead, they were trying to clear up some legal matter. How can people be so blind?

The church can get mixed up in legal matters when all it ought to see is human need and human suffering. Of what importance are these secondary matters of law so far as the father is concerned? Emerson asked the village physician at Concord about the health of the minister, Dr. Ripley. The doctor's reply was, "It's the most correct apoplexy I ever saw . . . all the symptoms are perfect." "Correct apoplexy and perfect symptoms" belong to the vocabulary of legalists, not of Christians.

Jesus walked among men and saw their need and their hurt.

Arguments about the situation interested him not at all. The truth is that arguments in most situations are not to the point and we ought to brush them aside in a hurry. No man was ever saved by being argued down. No man was ever healed because someone presented him with the right theory. Nearly always when you find an argument going on in a church, it is utterly useless to get involved or excited about it. All that arguments can do is so limited that the real work of the spirit of God is hardly ever preserved in their presence. Preachers, don't argue! See if there is not some way to relieve the pain.

WHEN FAITH FALLS SHORT

> **"I have faith," cried the boy's father; "help me where faith falls short."** 9:24

The RSV has it, "I believe, help my unbelief!" How much more pointed and specific is this version! The problem is primarily one of changing faith from a generality into a specific. We believe in general that he can do these things, but in this particular situation, where a son's whole life is at stake, how hard it is to believe that God will act here and now.

At a church meeting the preacher asked everybody who wanted to go to heaven to stand. Everybody stood except one man. The preacher was upset and said, "Brother, do you mean you don't want to go to heaven?" "No," said the man, of course I do." "Well then," he was asked, "why didn't you stand up?" "Oh," said the man, "I thought you were getting up a load for right now."

The fault of religious people is that they think too much of following the Lord's commandments at some future time. Faith is the kind of generality we accept as something that might happen some day to somebody else. The faith that has power is the faith that believes it can happen right now.

70

PRAYER POWER

> Then Jesus went indoors, and his disciples asked him privately, "Why could not we cast it out?" He said, "There is no means of casting out this sort but prayer." 9:28-29

Prayer is something we take very lightly, and we refer to it as something that will show the good will of the friend. How startling is Jesus' saying that there are some things so difficult that they can be accomplished only by prayer. George Bernard Shaw spoke of the low regard we have of prayer when he said, "Common people do not pray: they only beg." But Jesus is suggesting that prayer is a mighty power made available to us.

Oscar Wilde, in one of his plays, said, "When the gods wish to punish us they answer our prayers." This is nearer to the heart of the New Testament meaning than our easy-going passing off of prayer as a conventional gesture with no power. Jesus took prayer seriously and he was so impressed with its unlimited possibilities that he promised that everything could be done if we would only pray.

ECUMENICITY

> Jesus said, "Do not stop him; no one who does a work of divine power in my name will be able the next moment to speak evil of me. For he who is not against us is on our side." 9:39-40

The disciple spoke the word that the narrow sectarian always speaks. He criticized a man doing a good work because the man was not one of them. Jesus' word is one of tolerance and broad understanding. "For he who is not against us is on our side," is probably a proverb.

The ecumenical church, we are told, cannot come into being

until we find a common theology. It will never come that way. We get engaged in a task which seems to us part of the Lord's command. We will never say it the same way and perhaps we will not want to belong to the same organization. Unity is of the spirit, which is ultimate; without the spirit mere organizational oneness means very little.

One of the best Christians I ever knew was a man whose rough, uncultured way of putting things would have shocked most of my Christian friends. But in all the great issues in our contemporary life he was always on the side of Jesus Christ. It is for the preacher to interpret such saints to the church, and vice versa. We will save much time from useless bickering and we will be free to love one another. This fellowship the rebels of our time find hard to criticize.

AND GLADLY TEACH

> . . . he followed his usual practice and taught them.
>
> 10:1

The preacher is a teacher, unless he allows himself to become merely a loud voice emphasizing a few doctrines. There is nothing strange to us in human life, and the gospel manifests itself whenever a man brings the implication of the good news to a particular situation. No matter what drew the crowds to him, Jesus always used the opportunity to teach.

The preacher gives light to live by, and the congregation should feel as they leave his service that they have received new insight, new knowledge, and new perspective. Much of the teaching of Jesus was pointing out the spiritual and eternal meanings of some commonplace human experience, and the people heard Him gladly!

A man wrote to Chesterton and asked him to make his flamboyant imagery and his paradoxes more simple so that the people who had only a county school education could learn from him. Jesus never had this problem, for he spoke so simply and easily that plain men understood him. There was no place to hide in pious, murky words.

The author James Michener is one of the few men who has ever declined a dinner invitation to the White House. But he sent this letter to the President: "Dear Mr. President, I received your inviation three days after I had agreed to speak a few words at the dinner honoring the wonderful high school teacher who taught me how to write. I know you will not miss me at your dinner, but she might at hers." President Eiesenhower commented: "In his lifetime a man lives under fifteen or sixteen Presidents, but a really fine teacher comes into his life but rarely."

GOD UNLIMITED

> Jesus looked at them and said, "For men it is impossible, but not for God; everything is possible for God."   10:27

The things that we can do are limited. We can win wars, but we seemingly cannot establish peace. We can fight men, but we cannot fight ideas. This contemporary crisis reminds us again how limited our powers are. Things that mean change and progress all come from God.

The great Christians, while holding to faith in God, never abuse it by asking for foolish things nor by expecting God to be their errand boy. Dwight L. Moody was present with a group of wealthy laymen who were praying for the removal of a debt on their church. "Gentlemen," he said, "I don't think if I were you I would trouble the Lord in that matter." They could depend upon God to do what neither their wealth nor their talents could accomplish. The rich young ruler refused Jesus' advice, and the disciples were astounded that such a good young man was shut out from the kingdom. It is the power of God that can work the miracle of the changed heart. This is a sure sign of his presence and of his might. There is a legend that this young man, whom Jesus loved, was really the beloved disciple who wrote the Fourth Gospel.

WHEN FEAR BECOMES AWE

> ... and the disciples were filled with awe, while those who followed behind were afraid.   10:32

The New English Bible makes the point that the disciples were filled with awe while those who were following further back were afraid. What is the difference between fear and awe? In the early days of religion, holiness was a kind of fear, a sense of the taboo, a dangerous thing. It was the Old Testament which first associated the holy with the ethical. In this scene we have men who had only the sense of fear of something that was going to happen which they felt would be dangerous. But the disciples, although not comprehending all that was at stake, had been with Him enough to see that here was something beyond mere human courage. There was the great presence of God himself and they followed in awe. We might preach sometime on "Turning our fear into awe."

Joyce Cary writes, in *Except the Lord:* "My father had never lost his temper with us, never beaten us, but we had for him that feeling often described as fear, which is something quite different and far deeper than alarm. It was that sense which, without irreverence, I have thought to find expressed by the great evangelists when they speak of the fear of God." It is fear become awe.

74

NO ONE EXCUSED

> "For even the Son of Man did not come to be served
> but to serve, and to give up his life as a ransom for
> many."   10:45

Jesus pointed out to the two disciples who wanted the chief places in his kingdom that this was not possible for them or for himself. "For even the Son of Man" has to be a servant, He tells them, and play that part under God.

More than once Jesus identified himself with every man and claimed no special privilege over any of his followers. God has glorified him above all men, but he has not excused him from the hard discipline which He expects of all men. Said Athanasius in the fourth century: "He became what we are that He might make us what He is."

This is where Jesus takes his stand in the whole organization of the church. It is a great word to proclaim to people that "even the Son of Man did not come to be served but to serve." An evangelist, speaking of the Christian faith and Jesus Christ, was stopped by an angry voice from the crowd, "If your Jesus were here, I would spit on him." His only reply was, "It would not be the first time." The early Christians came to glory in their crucified leader and, instead of being an embarrassment, he became their chief glory.

TAKE HEART!

> Many of the people told him to hold his tongue; . . .
> so they called the blind man and said, "Take heart;
> stand up; he is calling you."   10:48-49

The blind beggar, Bartimaeus, hearing that Jesus was passing by on the road began to shout. The crowd told him to keep still, but Jesus wanted to see him. Suddenly the people were saying that he could take heart because Jesus was calling him.

The man who is desperate for help continues to call out whether the crowd likes it or not. Such people are usually referred to as "troublemakers" or rough individuals who are shouting about something that ought to be kept quiet. When a man is in need he does not have any hesitation, and he will not listen to those who counsel silence. But the great thing about the story is that when Jesus heard him and said, "Call him," then the crowd had a different word for the blind beggar. Now it was, "Take heart; stand up; he is calling you." And that is a wonderful thing indeed.

At the heart of the Christian experience is the conviction that we can seek Him only because, first of all, He is seeking us. One of the hardest things for us to learn is that God is more anxious to hear us than we are to ask. It is a great moment when a child discovers that is true of his father, and it is an even greater moment when we discover it through Jesus Christ.

HURRAY FOR JESUS

> "Blessings on the coming kingdom of our father David! Hosanna in the heavens!"   11:10

In the old Indian city of Cuzco, Peru, there appeared at Christmas time a neon sign, "Ole Jesus," which being interpreted, is "Hurray for Jesus." He prefers this over a cold, distant respect. The people who witnessed the triumphal entry were in this same exuberant mood, and the triumphant entrance seemed to them the first sign that the new kingdom was close at hand. "The coming kingdom" is always a reality for Christians. They live in the present, but they also live in the promise of greater things to come. We find this in St. Paul. Now and again he would stop and think of the wonderful promise ahead and break out in a poem of rejoicing. This is not just wishful thinking; it comes out of the experience of having a foretaste of the kingdom that is to be.

One of the paradoxical things about the kingdom of God is that it is present but it is also future. Those who follow Jesus possess it now. In some strange way which defies our logic, the coming kingdom has arrived. There is a sense in which the past and the future lose their sharp lines of distinction and combine into a kind of eternal now for the Christian.

THE WHOLE SCENE

> He entered Jerusalem and went into the temple, where he looked at the whole scene. . . .   11:11

The New English Bible makes this passage very modern. He took a hasty glance at the whole situation, or we might say he made a survey. He walked through the temple and appraised that religious agency. A little later he made his judgment, that the house of prayer had been turned into a den of thieves. This was the part of the scene which disturbed him the most, for what the religious institution should have been doing, it had denied.

Jesus was always doing this, so that whatever he said has a universal note. Churchmen often confine themselves to one segment of the community or one point of view. They only know part of it. This is the politician's difficulty also. Over against these partial views which are so characteristic of so many parts of our society, the church ought to see the whole scene. This is the contribution which Christians can make to their society. Sometimes they are the only ones who can point out something which the business community or the financial community have overlooked. In Jesus' rather hurried glance He took in all the issues at stake, all the crying needs and all the deep seeking of people who could not even phrase it for themselves.

NO THOROUGHFARE

> ... he would not allow anyone to use the temple
> court as a thoroughfare for carrying goods.   11:16

A friend of mine many years ago visited a Greek Orthodox
Church in San Francisco and talked with the priest. Noticing
that there were no chairs, he asked the priest why they did not
provide more comfort for their worshipers. Said the priest,
"There are only two positions a man ought to assume when he
is in the presence of God. One is on his knees praying, 'Lord
be merciful to me, a sinner,' and the other is on his feet saying,
'Lord, here am I, send me.'" The church is not the place for
bargaining, and the temple is not the place to transport your
goods.

THEY WERE AFRAID OF HIM

> ... for they were afraid of him, because the whole
> crowd was spellbound by his teaching.   11:18

Palestine in the first century was not a democracy. It was a part
of an empire that never hesitated to crush opposition. Yet the
authorities were afraid of Jesus because his teaching held the
people spellbound.

Joseph Conrad wrote that if he had the right word he could
move the world. People are not moved by the right arguments,
and not even by the right law. But when the right word finds
them, they are confronted by something that can change their
lives. This was why the authorities were afraid of Jesus.

As I write there is facing me a picture of Albert Schweitzer,
which he autographed when I visited him a few years ago.
There is also that famous word that he spoke about Jesus, "He
speaks to us the same word: 'Follow thou me!' and sets us to
the tasks which he has to fulfill for our time. He commands.

And to those who obey him, whether they be wise or simple, he will reveal himself in the toils, the conflicts, the sufferings which they shall pass through in his fellowship, and, as an ineffable mystery, they shall learn in their own experience who he is." Something of this power came through to the crowd in Jesus' presence: the authorities "were afraid of him."

CRAFTY QUESTIONS

> He saw how crafty their question was. . . .   12:15

The best lawyers were constantly trying to find some way to embroil Jesus in contradictions. What a commentary it is on his society that those who could not dispose of him in any other way tried to destroy him through "crafty questions"!

The preacher knows such people, and in student discussion groups there will be some wise boy or girl who will try to entrap the speaker. The politician soon learns that speaking frankly and openly is fraught with danger. Usually the politician takes refuge in obscurities and generalities, or else he keeps his silence.

Donald Soper, one of England's great preachers, was in the habit of speaking at Hyde Park on Sunday afternoon. He had all kinds of questions thrown at him. One of them was, "What is the shape of the soul when it leaves the body?" Soper quickly replied, "Oblong," and went on to his next point. Jesus dealt with crafty questions many times. He spoke simply, but he had great intelligence and his answers have stood the test for all these years.

PRAYING FOR EFFECT

> "These are the men who eat up the property of widows, while they say long prayers for appearance' sake. . . .   12:40

The people who are most condemned by Jesus are the hypocrites. He could not stand hypocrisy, and he was particularly severe with those who were hypocritical for some religious reason. He hated phonies. In this verse we have an example of those who rob widows and then "say long prayers for appearance' sake." We need to preach once in awhile on what people do for the sake of appearances. Long prayers are bad enough in any case, but when they are done to impress people, they are unbearable.

A Boston newspaper referred to a minister's prayer as "one of the most eloquent ever addressed to a Boston audience." The notice was all the comment needed. There is a story about William Lyons Phelps saying grace at home. His wife commented, "William, I didn't hear a word you said." He replied, "My dear, I was not addressing you." Prayers that are addressed to God are simple, direct, and, oftentimes, rough in their construction, but they come from the heart.

THE TRULY GENEROUS

> ". . . for those others who have given had more than enough, but she, with less than enough, has given all that she had to live on."   12:44

I was in a church in the east a few years ago, and the minister told me that while he had very few people attending, the church had more money than it knew how to spend wisely. A huge endowment fund had been left through the years and the income from it could not possibly be spent intelligently. He said to me, "It is a very hard thing to preach in this church on giving." While it must have been a great relief not to worry about money for the budget, that minister's problem was a greater one so far as ministering to the spiritual life of his people was concerned.

We are in a similar situation in our civilization. This is an affluent nation, and we have too much. But we are a people that spend billions of dollars on a war and yet does not have enough money to minister to some of the poverty-stricken areas in our ghettos. The giving of the poor widow should be our text when we talk to our congregation on giving.

I have a new church in a new community in my area. The finance committee met one afternoon to decide what they could do to meet their obligations. While they were in session, the minister was called to the door by an old man who was living by himself on social security. The old man had ridden twenty miles on his bicycle to say that he had just received the church paper and read that they needed payment on pledges just as soon as possible. He had come down to pay his money, three dollars. Then he left to ride back uphill to his shack. When the minister came in and told the committee about it, each one of them made a contribution immediately and they went out to have the greatest financial campaign they had ever had in that church. The example of the poor widow is better than the cleverest letter of appeal that any advertising agency can ever write.

I PLEDGE ALLEGIANCE

"All will hate you for your allegiance to me. . . ."
13:13

Pledging "allegiance" to Christ is a phrase rich with meanings. It goes back to feudal times, when a man owed allegiance to his lord. It was a personal thing. Today we pledge allegiance to the nation and to the flag, with the understanding that we owe our country something personal. Allegiance to Christ means allegiance to his kingdom, just as allegiance to America means loyalty to the values of America.

We pledge allegiance to the church whenever we join. That means we are part of it, not just until a minister comes that we don't like or until the church sponsors something we disapprove. Our allegiance is something final; it is a relationship which the church can count on no matter what happens.

And Jesus warned us that we will be hated for our allegiance to him. The time comes, of course, when we have to choose. The Christian has pledged allegiance to Christ, and this ultimate loyalty carries him through all the suffering, the insult, and the betrayals which are to be expected he will share with his Lord.

At 11:55 a.m., October 21, 1805, Horatio Nelson sent out signal 16: "England expects that every man will do his duty." Admiral Cuthbert Collingwood, who had started the Battle of Trafalgar by bringing The Royal Sovereign into action, grumbled, "I wish Nelson would stop signalling." Constant affirmation is not essential, only the assurance that come what may, we are committed.

TROUBLEMAKERS FOR THE WRONG REASONS

> "Why must you make trouble for her? ... She has done what lay in her power. ..." 14:6-8

In one sense the criticism was just. The perfume could have been sold instead of being poured on Jesus' head. But the critics forget that such money will not be used for the poor and it will not be available for any other cause whatsoever. Every building campaign in a church always has to face the criticism of people who say the money should be spent for missions or social action. All the time the minister knows that the money will not be used for these other purposes because it will not be available.

Is money wasted when it is spent on some beautiful thing for which there is no practical use? The bridegroom soon learns that money spent for flowers or some foolish unexpected gift is never wasted. It adds something to the whole marriage relationship that does more to keep it stable and eternal than any amount of money which might have been saved. Or if some unexpected gift from a friend is received that has no practical use, we never think how much better it would have been if he had put the money to some other use. He made an investment in friendship, and this is one of the best investments any man can make.

Jesus said that she had done what was in her power to do. That is all that he ever expects from us. There are important things within our power. The gallant gesture, the act of love, the act of devotion, the indication of deep concern and respect, all are within our power. In the end they are more important than some of the most spectacular things we think we would do if we had the money. Remember the little acts of grace.

NO GUARANTEE

> The third time he came and said to them, "Still sleeping? Still taking your ease? Enough! The hour has come. The Son of Man is betrayed to sinful men. Up, let us go forward! My betrayer is upon us."
>
> 14:41-42

William James wrote, "Suppose that the world's author put the case to you before Creation, saying: 'I am going to make a world not certain to be saved, a world the perfection of which shall be conditioned merely, the condition that each several agent does his own *level best*. I offer you the chance of taking part in such a world. Safety, you see, is unwarranted. It is a real adventure, with real danger, yet it may win through.... Will you join the procession? Will you trust

yourself and trust the other agents enough to face the risk?' "
Now this all comes to focus in the scene of the betrayal of
Jesus Christ. What a risk was involved here and how easily
everything could have gone wrong! The disciples fell asleep
and now their Lord has been betrayed into the hands of
sinners.

Studdert-Kennedy, who was a chaplain in the First World
War, captured this sense of the Christian faith as well as anybody I know. He said: "It demands a risk of life far beyond
what we can prove." Jesus played down the idea of proof and
put his emphasis upon risk and daring. The appeal of the
gospel is to the young and the brave. We must never let the
timid who prefer security to any splendid possibility have
their way with the gospel. They must, on the contrary, believe it just as Mark told it, following the One whose word
in this great crucial moment of His life was, "Up, let us go
forward! My betrayer is upon us."

MOCKERY

> When they had finished their mockery, they . . .
> dressed him in his own clothes.   15:20

Mockery is the hardest treatment to endure. This is the way
we show our contempt and this is the way we try to inflict
the deepest humiliation upon another. In no other place in
the gospel does the innate dignity of Jesus shine forth with
such splendor as in this experience of enduring mockery.

We mock our Lord in more subtle ways. The horrible
mockery of the Prince of Peace is war. How much we will
have to answer for by our attempts to dress Him in the
national uniform and send Him forth to kill! What rank
amateurs the soldiers of the governor were compared to us
when it came to mocking Jesus!

How we mock Him when we cut our sympathy from our

brothers and withhold all generosity from the needy. We who name His name forget that when we deal with a needy person, we are dealing with Him, and so mock His love.

His simple teaching about our neighbors we have mocked and blasphemed when we shut off the privileges of our communities from those whose color is different from ours. The two thousand years of Christian history are full of our mockery of the Lord. It was not ended in a few hours or even in a few years. He is mocked not only by His enemies, but by His friends. The old spiritual has it, "Were you there when they crucified my Lord?" Well, we were certainly there when the military mocked him.

Does God mock men? Only by giving us what we think we want. Said Austin O'Malley, a writer of the early part of this century: "God shows his contempt for wealth by the kind of person he selects to receive it."

PRESSED INTO SERVICE

> A man called Simon, from Cyrene, the father of Alexander and Rufus, was passing by on his way ... and they pressed him into service to carry his cross.   15:21

This unusual detail about "a man called Simon" indicates that the community where the gospel was written knew Alexander and Rufus. Perhaps it was in North Africa, where there were substantial Jewish settlements, or perhaps this was the Rufus that Paul mentioned in his letter to the Romans. But it seems fairly sure that Alexander and Rufus were early Christians, and one can imagine them bearing testimony that they knew something about the crucifixion because, "Our father carried His cross."

The criminal to be executed usually carried his own cross,

but because Jesus was exhausted they compelled a passer-by to do this chore. What was Simon's reaction, and did he do it gladly or sullenly?

When we are pressed into service we usually resent it. We can think of a dozen reasons why we should not have been forced into this situation. But consider the times when we have been "pressed into service" for Jesus Christ which have turned out to be the great moments of our lives. God has a way of sometimes forcing us into a duty which is a doorway leading us into a bigger world. We are sometimes drafted into greatness without knowing why or how until long after the occasion is ended. God leads us in ways we have not chosen. John Wesley went to the little chapel on Aldersgate street rather unwillingly. It was in that place where his heart was strangely warmed and the new life was made clear to him. It is sometimes the handicap or the sickness that makes possible the great experience which otherwise would have been missed. There are times when we have been forced into accepting obligations we would have escaped if possible, only to find that these have been the turning points in our lives. If we are sensitive and observant enough, we shall probably discover that by pressing us into service God makes it possible for us to receive His greatest gifts. The happiest and most wonderful people I have known have been those who have had burdens thrust upon them and by carrying them have found joy.

SEEING IS BELIEVING?

> "If we see that, we shall believe."   15:32

It is clear that men are not brought to faith by miraculous signs, and Jesus refused to make them. Such signs are quickly forgotten, or else men ask, "I wonder how that was done?" The wonder workers never inspire us either to believe or to live with greater nobility. Our Lord faced this temptation and disposed of it early in his ministry. But he was annoyed by people who made the claim that if he would just do something miraculous, they would believe.

Christians can take a lesson from this for themselves. Men are not convinced of our saintliness, because they think we have been excused from suffering. They are convinced only by the life of service and devotion which takes the suffering every man has to endure and transforms it into something wonderful beyond our understanding.

One day Herbert Spencer, the philosopher, was traveling in a railroad carriage. He sat opposite a poor laborer busy eating his lunch. Spencer wrote, "His mode of eating was so brutish as to attract my attention and fill me with disgust; a disgust which verged into anger." But after awhile the laborer finished his meal and sat quietly. Spencer wrote, "Then I was struck by the woebegone expression of his face. Years of suffering were registered on it . . . and while I gazed on the sad eyes and the deeply marked lines I began to realize the life of misery through which he had passed." Suffering finally reaches even the most sophisticated and intelligent with its quiet patience.

THE CONCLUSION

> They said nothing to anybody, for they were afraid.
> 16:8

This is where the original Gospel of Mark ends, although other endings were added to later versions. This is what Jesus does to human life. The last word "for they were afraid" is changed into a testimony to the greatness and splendor of what he has done for men and what they can now expect.

What is the last word that can be spoken of a man's life? Fear? For a vast number of people it must be fear, because with nothing else to experience and so nothing more to hope for, life comes to the end in frustration and despair. At the signing of the Declaration of Independence, Benjamin Franklin commented on how hard it was to differentiate between a picture of a sunrise and a sunset. He dared to hope, he said, that what they had done would prove to be a rising sun and not its setting. That is what Christ does for human life. The word of fear changes into the word of triumph and hope. He changes our sunsets into sunrise.

It is this final word that sums up either the tragedy or the victory of life. In Robert Southey's poem, "The Battle of Blenheim," old Kaspar tries to explain the whole business to young Peterkin and little Wilhelmine. He says that the English put the French to rout, but what they killed each other for, he does not know. And then comes these two lines:

> But everybody said, quoth he,
> That 'twas a famous victory.

So many human endeavors end up like that, and so many battles are just as hard to justify. So many human lives are lost so uselessly, as in Southey's summing up of the famous battle.

FAITH AND MIRACLES

"Faith will bring with it these miracles. . . ."   16:17

This is an important verse. It reverses what we conceive to be the usual order. We think that we will see the miracle and then we will have faith. But it is written here that if we have faith, then we may expect the miracles. And as George Bernard Shaw pointed out in his play, "Saint Joan," anything that creates faith is a miracle.

Discoveries and accomplishments are made by people who

go forth not knowing exactly where they are or where they are going. Abraham is a symbol of the Hebrew people. Great achievements all begin with a man pioneering into the unknown. It is this faith in God that works miracles.

It has been written that every great age is an age of faith and every poor age is an age of doubt. This does not mean that if we believe everything, we become great, but only that when our minds are open to what God can do and what God has done, we are made aware of our constant dwelling in the midst of miracle.

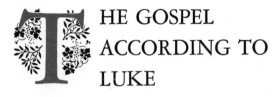

THE GOSPEL ACCORDING TO LUKE

INTRODUCTION

> "The spirit of the Lord is upon me because he has
>   anointed me;
> he has sent me to announce good news to the poor,
> to proclaim release for prisoners and recovery of
>   sight for the blind;
> to let the broken victims go free,
> to proclaim the year of the Lord's favor."   4:18–19

When I read the Gospel of St. Luke in the New English Bible,
I recalled the word of a literary critic, who said that Luke's
gospel was the most beautiful book he had ever read.

Luke addressed his gospel to Theophilus, who was probably
a well-to-do Roman interested in Christianity. The first volume
is about Jesus Christ and the events centered in his life. Then
Luke wrote another volume, which we call the Acts of the
Apostles, telling the story of the early church after Jesus'
death. Luke was a physician who traveled with Paul on some
of his journeys. When the author begins to use "we" instead
of the third person, he is telling of the things he actually saw
and experienced. The gospel of St. Luke was written in the
last quarter of the first century, and it reflects a writer of
sensitive spirit and loving heart.

We note first that Luke emphasized in this portrait Jesus'
blindness to the artificial distinctions which men set up in
society. The man whose father and grandfather were honored
pillars of our community has a distinct advantage over the

stranger or the newcomer. Wealth plays a part in our distinctions, and no one can honestly claim that a millionaire receives the same justice as a vagrant. The poor do get less consideration than the rich.

Jesus was at home with the Samaritans, who were looked down upon by the Jews. It is in this gospel that we read that unforgettable story of the man coming down from Jerusalem to Jericho who fell in with thieves. His plight was ignored by a priest and Levite, but a Samaritan bound up his wounds and took him to an inn.

In this gospel we see the love of Christ for the neglected and despised. The church has never done as much as it might have done for these, even though through the years Christians have tried to bear witness of service to the forgotten and neglected. Luke tells us about the grace of the Lord Jesus, who has love and concern for those the world despises and neglects. When Harry Golden's mother died, he remembered the time she had given him five dollars to buy groceries for the family. On the way to the store he stopped to play in a vacant lot with some boys, and he lost the money. He searched desperately but he could not find it. He sat on a bench in the park wondering how he dared to go home and tell his mother that he had lost the money which meant so much to his poor family. Finally it got dark, and he went home crying and sobbed out the story to his mother. She put her arm around him and said, "Harry, better than giving it to a doctor." In the kindness and concern and grace, she had given the boy something he could never forget.

But another theme runs through this book, and that is the austere, hard emphasis on the Lordship of Christ. Most of us began our acquaintance with the church as children, when we learned of a gentle Jesus. It is a true word about him, but it is not the whole picture though many of us never go beyond it. Some think of Jesus as an other worldly poet who said some rather nice things about loving your enemy. We agree that we will serve him if we have the time. We put the church last on the list when it comes to sacrifice and faithfulness. In Luke's gospel we are brought face to face with One who was the Lord of all life and of all men.

From this gospel comes the idea, finally, that at the heart of the universe there is a divine concern. We know so little about God, but in Jesus Christ we have the necessary clues. The grandson of Ernest Renan knocked at a priest's door one time and said rather arrogantly, "Come outside. I want to talk to you about a problem." But the priest replied to the young man, "You come inside and let me talk to you about your sins." It is this hard and austere word we need to hear.

T. R. Glover, one of the fine Christian scholars of the early part of this century, was walking home one night with a friend. Gospel of Luke we have a revelation of what we ought to do Suddenly he stopped and said, "I do not give tuppence for the preacher who tells me what my duty is but I bow before the man who can tell me from whence cometh my help." In the or what our obligations are, but we also have a portrait of the Incarnation of God who not only makes clear what we must do but in whose love for us we find our succor and our redemption.

EPITAPH

"...and many will be glad that he was born...." 1:14

A good epitaph! The minister has to conduct many funerals and speak about the deceased. This is a great privilege if the man has been a Christian or a good man. Sometimes, however, it presents a real difficulty in trying to find something to be said of a man who has little about him worth saying. We cannot say that he made a lot of money or that he was a great business success as something appropriate at a funeral service.

Suddenly we realize that so many of the things which are accounted worthy of biography under ordinary circumstances seem to have no place here. This word, however, says it perfectly and completely; no man could ask for a better expression of appreciation than that many were glad he had been born.

In 1954, Dr. Charles L. Wallis published a most interesting book on American epitaphs, which he called *Stories on Stone.* In his foreword he says that an eighteenth-century volume for epitaph-writers gave the advice that (1) "the praise bestowed on the dead should be restrained within the bounds of truth," (2) "the epitaph should edify or admonish the reader," (3) "the serious reflections should be written in as lively and striking a manner as possible," and (4) the epitaph should be brief. This word of the angel to Zechariah seems to me to include all these marks of a good epitaph. It might be a good idea to ask ourselves just how many people will be glad that we were born when we leave this life.

TIMING

> ". . . though at their proper time my words will be
> proved true."   1:20

Consider the importance of timing. The comedian gets his effect as much by his timing as he does by what he says. The poet opens up the dark mysteries of life by the right timing of his right word. Great drama states the idea or shows the point just at the right moment. How important this is to the preacher, for the effective sermon is dependent upon the right timing. God's sense of timing is terrific.

HER NAME WAS MARY

... the girl's name was Mary.   1:27

The father of John the Baptist had his vision and his message from the angel in the holy place of the temple. But the mother of Jesus had her experience in an ordinary place in Nazareth. Nobody knew her, and she was not associated with a religious establishment. The writer simply said that her name was Mary. In this announcement to one who was to be the mother of our Lord was revealed the greatness about to be bestowed upon her. All that was asked of her was obedience.

Our Catholic brethren have emphasized the honored place which the Virgin Mary has held. But the word used here is not necessarily translated "virgin," although sometimes it was used with that meaning. Ordinarily, however, as the New English Bible makes clear, the word means just "girl," one not yet married, and in her case, one who was engaged. This is one of the great verses in the Bible for me, because I married a girl named Mary. It is a beautiful name and it speaks to me of how a man has received the favor of God if a girl named Mary accepts him. This is miracle enough.

YOUR SERVANT, LORD

"I am the Lord's servant; as you have spoken, so be it.
1:38

Mary was in the midst of an experience that overwhelmed her with its wonder and grandeur. One thing that seemed clear to her was that the Lord had spoken, and in humility she replied that she would obey.

Probably one of the hardest lessons for us to learn is that surrendering to God does not make us less, but more. Nations do not learn it, and in following their own wills they go on to destruction. Oriental religions often have this strong strain of humility running through them. It seems merely passive and weak to the Western world, but Christianity centered in Jesus Christ shows us that surrender is really victory.

TRIUMPH OF THE HUMBLE

> the arrogant of heart and mind he has put to rout,
> he has brought down monarchs from their thrones,
> but the humble have been lifted high.   1:51–52

This beautiful psalm, known as the Magnificat, interrupts the narrative, but it is in harmony with the whole spirit of the birth of Jesus in the midst of the greatest empire the world had seen up to that time. Out of an insignificant tribe down at the eastern end of the Mediterranean Sea came this great affirmation of God's vindication of the poor and humble. Jesus is the inheritor of Israel's long tradition of God's power. Against the might of the state, God's power gives the triumph to the humble and the poor. The birth of Jesus was the beginning of a revolution against special privilege and the arrogance of the rich.

Women find special understanding and respect from Jesus. This does not seem so extraordinary to us, but in the first century women were chattels and property. It was unusual to pay them honor and courtesy. In the Magnificat, Mary rejoices in God by whom "the humble have been lifted high."

POTENTIAL UNLIMITED

> All who heard it were deeply impressed and said,
> "What will this child become?" For indeed the hand
> of the Lord was upon him.   1:66

The birth of John was accompanied by wonderful signs. The people heard about this and asked, "What will this child become?" The possibilities were simply unlimited, because "the hand of the Lord was upon him."

When a minister baptizes a baby, something of this same feeling is in his heart. He holds the infant and reflects to himself, "What do I hold here in my hands? What shall this boy or girl mean to our nation, our society?" Infinite possibilities are here, for we have learned that when God wants to do something great, he usually does it through a person. Infant baptism gives the congregation and the minister of the church a moment to contemplate this question: "What will this child become?"

On the one-hundredth anniversary of Abraham Lincoln's birth, February 1909, H. T. Webster drew a striking picture. Two Kentucky frontiersmen met on a snow-covered path, the trees bare and gaunt against the winter sky. They paused to visit. One of them asked, "Any news from down at the village, Ezry?" His friend replied, "Well, Squire McLean's gone to Washington to see Madison swore in, and old Spellman tells me that Bonaparte fellow has captured most of Spain. What's new out here, neighbor?" "Oh," said the other one, "Nuthin' atall except for a new baby down at Tom Lincoln's. Nuthin' ever happens out here." But when people believe that God's hand is upon a child, they know that something *can* happen out here.

What a word this is for parents! What a responsibility is laid upon them for the care and development of their children! Chesterton once said he could not understand how it was considered a great career to teach other people's children and not very important to teach one's own. Every new generation is a promise fresh from God.

GOOD NEWS

> "Do not be afraid; I have good news for you: there is great joy coming to the whole people. . . ." 2:10

Preachers, like other Christians, let their temptations and their past experiences influence their interpretation of the gospel. The naturally solemn, gloomy individual tends to have a somber religious outlook. But as John Wesley said, "Sour godliness is the devil's religion."

We must remember that Christians are recipients of "good news." The preacher must not forget that basic fact in every sermon he preaches. It carries the ringing triumphal note that God has done something for us which can only be called good news for all the people: He has given us His Son.

CHARACTER, PATIENCE, AND THE HOLY SPIRIT

> This man was upright and devout, one who watched and waited for the restoration of Israel, and the Holy Spirit was upon him. 2:25

This is a description of Simeon, and it could be set down as the proper description of the Christian man. In the first place, he was a man of character and good behavior, or as the New English Bible puts it, "He was upright and devout." Nothing good can come out of a man until he is first established in his character.

In the second place, he was a man of expectancy and patience, or, as the verse puts it, "One who watched and waited." Impatient men are affected by every passing wind of opinion. We have a great hope, a great expectancy, and we must have courage to wait for God's fulfillment of His promise.

The third mark of such a man is that "the Holy Spirit was upon him." A man with the Holy Spirit in his heart is strengthened and maintained by a sense of the living presence of God.

THE OLD MAN AND THE BABY

> "This day, Master, thou givest thy servant his
>   discharge in peace;
>   now thy promise is fulfilled.
> For I have seen with my own eyes
> the deliverance which thou hast made ready in full view
>   of all the nations:
> a light that will be a revelation to the heathen,
>   and glory to thy people Israel."   2:29–32

This poem of Simeon's is reminiscent of Isaiah's words, and no doubt the old man knew the Book of Isaiah. Simeon's words represent a sermon for us.

He had been given a promise, and he had waited expectantly to see it fulfilled. Now he rejoiced. He was ready to depart, for the guarantee of God had been fulfilled in the baby who was to be the Messiah. There is something splendid in the old man's confessing his willingness to die now that he has seen the future in this new life of the baby.

Simeon added that this is to be for all the nations and a revelation for the heathen. This is not something to be hidden or kept for one group or even one nation. It comes through the Jews, but its meaning is for everybody. So Simeon rejoiced in it as God's gift, not just to himself and to his own people, but to all the world.

Simeon closed his poem rejoicing that it should be "glory to thy people Israel." The chosen people are to give and to share. Thus at the beginning of the story we see an old man's vision of the universal nature of Jesus Christ and His way of life. Simeon rejoiced that his people had been chosen to bring this gift to the world.

LOOKING FOR A MIRACLE

> ... and she talked about the child to all who were
> looking for the liberation of Jerusalem.   2:38

Anna gave the second prophetic witness that Jesus was the Messiah. She spent her whole time at the temple and she told people about Jesus. But the verse suggests that she could only be sure of a hearing from those "who were looking for the liberation of Jerusalem." Only those who were expecting his coming were in a mood to understand what she had to say.

What a great thing it is to live expectantly! I remember the grandmother who told me of her little grandson helping her with the dishes one night and trying to explain what the Sunday School teacher has been telling him. "It is sort of like this, Grandma," he said. "We are walking along. We come around a corner and suddenly there's God." He had the heart of it; that is a good way to describe the Christian faith. There was the little boy whose neighbors invited him to come along with their own children to a circus. He was so filled with the wonder and glory of it that when he came home, he tried his best to tell his grandmother about it. She had often taken him to prayer meetings with her and he finally summed it all up by saying, "I'll tell you one thing, Grandma. If you have ever been to a circus, you will never want to go to another prayer meeting." It is to that spirit that the prophetess spoke.

AUTHORITY

> Then he went back with them to Nazareth, and
> continued to be under their authority.... 2:51

Most parents now are finding authority a problem in dealing with their children. If Jesus were speaking in the modern mood, he would never mention being under the authority of his parents. Yet, after the breaking away from the group and losing himself in the temple, he again joined the family and placed himself under the authority of his mother and father.

His whole life reflects an understanding of the true nature of authority. The gospel says he spoke with authority, but the gospel also makes it clear that he never tried to force his teaching upon the people through any external pressure. He learned from the authority of his parents the only way to win the hearts of men.

The authority of the home is based upon the assurance of young people that their parents love them. The authority of the state is only real when it springs from dedication to the great purposes by which the nation lives. The authority of the church is never established by a pope or a council. All of these institutions must believe in freedom and we obey them because their truth has found us.

ROAD BUILDERS

> "Every ravine shall be filled in,
> and every mountain and hill levelled...." 3:5

These words are from Isaiah, and they describe the preaching and witness of John the Baptist. Some years ago, at a theological seminary, a professor told me that he thought he had discovered the earliest literary reference to the Greek term "episcopas," which is the word we translate as "bishop." When I asked him what it had meant, he replied, "A bishop originally was a straw boss of a road gang." I told him it was about the best definition of my job that I had heard. What is the position of a Christian, or a minister, or even of a bishop? Isaiah saw the picture of the road builder, smoothing out the rough places and leveling the high places to make the way straight and safe. John was preparing the way for Jesus, and it was his job to make a highway for God through the wilderness.

BE SPECIFIC

> Soldiers on service also asked him, "And what of us?" To them he said, "No bullying; no blackmail; make do with your pay!"　　　　　3:14

John's preaching exhibited one of the main characteristics of a good sermon. It was specific, and not general. If we talk in generalities we shall seldom get into any trouble, but we will never move the congregation to any action.

Each man has to see what the gospel demands of him in his own situation. Every job has some special temptations, and every man needs help in interpreting the gospel for himself in his own particular place. Soldiers are subject to temptations of bullying and blackmailing and trying to make an extra dollar through pressure. John told them exactly what his teaching meant for them.

A man who had just put down a new sidewalk looked out the window and saw the neighbor children making marks in it. He was angry and said some very rude things to them. Another neighbor inquired: "Don't you like children?" "In general," was the response, "but not in the concrete." It is the concrete demand that makes us know whether we are for it or against it. If you want a decision, do not deal in generalities.

GREAT EXPECTATIONS

The people were on the tiptoe of expectation. . . .

3:15

What effect does the gospel have on people? We have been
through a period when it was supposed to bring us comfort and
quiet our fears. But that tells more about the mood we have
been in than it does about the gospel itself. Luke says that
there was in the air of the first century a feeling of expectation.
They were on tiptoe, and this new prophet found them ready to
listen to his hard words because they were aware of their great
need.

People living on tiptoe are looking for something. The dull
are not expectant. Consider our services of worship. The worst
thing, and the truest thing, we can say about many of them is
that they are dull and lifeless. We do not expect anything to
happen, and we are not disappointed. Let a congregation be
expectant and the liturgy comes to life.

The great periods of power in the history of Christianity have
been the times of expectation. You can define the gospel with
the title of Dickens' novel: *Great Expectations.*

GET MAD!

**At these words the whole congregation were in-
furiated.**

4:28

John Wesley was questioning one of his intinerant preachers
who had returned from a preaching journey. Wesley asked him
if he had converted anybody and the man confessed sadly that
he had not. Then asked John Wesley, "Did you make anybody
angry?" And when he said no to that question, Wesley thought
he was hopeless.

Yet when you turn to the gospels there are not many references to the anger of our Lord. In the third chapter of St. Mark, fifth verse, we read: ". . . and, looking round at them with anger and sorrow at their obstinate stupidity, he said to the man, 'Stretch out your arm.' " (Mark 3:5). That men should allow an overconcern with rules to interfere with mercy and healing roused his anger. But he was the Prince of Peace.

A mother in Stockholm, Sweden, told me that her own children and their friends, ages eight to eleven, became concerned because so much money was being spent for war when there were millions of hungry children in the world. They formed an organization called "The Young Angry Ones." At their insistence she wrote a letter to the Prime Minister and asked for an appointment for them. To her surprise he agreed to see them, and he talked with them for half an hour about the problem of hungry children. Out of their anger these children brought to the attention of their elders the foolishness of our ways. There is such a thing as constructive anger. We should never lose it. The blasé generation that assumes that nothing can be done and everything will go along in the same old way is lost. Remember Gerald Green's novel, *The Last Angry Man*. It is a sad day for society when men no longer get angry at injustice.

IF YOU SAY SO

> "Master, we were hard at work all night and caught nothing at all; but if you say so, I will let down the nets."
> 5:5

Simon Peter was saying, "We have fished all night and there are no fish anywhere around here. Your suggestion is useless. Nevertheless, if you say so, I will try it again."

Whenever we come into a dry period when no one seems to respond to the evangelism of the church, we redouble our efforts with every new trick we can scheme up. The command of Jesus does not strike us as being very realistic. We sometimes bring ourselves to try once more, but without enthusiasm. We wonder if his methods work in our time, and if the church perhaps has come to the end. Yet if we have the courage to follow our Lord's direction, once again the result may be as staggering as it was to Simon Peter.

WE NEED LONELY PLACES

> **And from time to time he would withdraw to lonely places for prayer.**   5:16

Colin Fletcher walked the whole length of the Grand Canyon and recounted the experience in his book, *The Man Who Walked Through Time*. In one place he writes, "Now, every sunlit desert morning has a magic moment. It may come at five o'clock, at seven, or at eleven, depending on the weather and the season. But it comes. If you are in the right mood at the right time you are suddenly aware that the desert's countless cogs have meshed. That the world has crystallized into vivid focus. And you respond. You hold your breath or fall into a reverie or spring to your feet, according to the day and the mood." There used to be more of these moments available for people than there are now. But Fletcher has written of those great moments of insight which come out of prayer, though he was writing about the Grand Canyon. Jesus had such insights, and that is why it was so necessary for him to visit those lonely places of the desert from time to time.

We would be well-advised to pass up some of the night club roundups and some of the vacations which simply throw us among more people than we meet at home, and seek some solitary place. It would help us all year. Indeed, our task is to find some substitute near at home for the lonely places, or the desert. We are not to consider our prayer life as something on display, as the Pharisees, past and present, tend to do. The main thing is to shut ourselves off from confusion that we may hear the still small voice. Prayer is listening.

YOU'LL NEVER BELIEVE IT

> They were all lost in amazement and praised God; filled with awe they said, "You would never believe the things we have seen today."   5:26

"On the afternoon of 24 May 1883 there was an interview between Beatrice Potter, afterwards Beatrice Webb, and Eleanor Marx, daughter of Karl Marx, in the refreshment room of the British Museum. They argued over the rightness of ridiculing Christianity. 'We think the Christian religion,' said Eleanor Marx, 'an immoral illusion, and we wish to use any argument to persuade the people that it is false. Ridicule appeals to the people we have to deal with, in much greater force than any amount of serious logical argument.... We want to make them [the working classes] disregard the mythical next world and live for this world, and insist on having what will make it pleasant to them.' Beatrice Potter found it useless, she wrote, to argue with one who had no idea of the beauty of the Christian religion, and read the gospels as the gospel of damnation." (*The Victorian Church, Part II,* by Owen Chadwick, Oxford University Press, 1970).

Over against the prosaic routine of many a Christian preacher there is this startling verse in the gospel. Jesus had just confronted the Pharisees and met their accusation of blasphemy with his command to the paralytic that he stand up and walk. Then, wrote Luke, after they saw this happen, they said to those who had not been there, "You would never believe the things we have seen today." The gospel had become to them power, love, and miracle.

OLD IS BEST

> "And no one after drinking old wine wants new; for
> he says, 'The old wine is good.' "   5:39

Many a preacher will feel it is time to say a good word for the
old, and here it is. There are some things that are no good until
they have been aged. Nobody desires new wine if he can have
the old. Age makes some things better, not worse. Consider a
few of these.

There is love. New love has excitement, but old love has a
value that casts a golden glow over all life. Agatha Christie,
who writes mysteries, married an archeologist. A friend asked
her what it was like to be married to such a man. "Wonderful,"
said Miss Christie, "the older I get the more he finds me interesting." And there is friendship. Does anybody want to argue that
a new friendship is automatically better than an old one?
Nothing can compare with old friends, and as the years go by
they become more wonderful than ever. Or you might think of
character. Character by its very definition has to have some years
back of it. Consider human life. The young man may announce
high aims and goals, but the old man rests in the wonder and
miracle of all that he has tested and tried.

YOU HAVE HAD IT

> "But alas for you who are rich; you have had your
> time of happiness."   6:24

I attended a meeting where the leader, in describing a program
which he thought the church ought to adopt, said simply, "I am
too old a man to prepare for the past." A good many of the
things we spend our time on are attempts to prepare for yesterday. Jesus speaks to that point of view in this beatitude. The
worst thing he could say about the rich was, "You have had

your time of happiness." We must be wise enough in our own personal lives to guard against taking unto ourselves only treasures of yesterday. We must not live in the past tense. Jesus implies that this is what the pagans do.

The test of the cause we are asked to support is whether or not it contains the seeds of tomorrow. No matter what our age, we are all too old to make our lives a service only to yesterday. The expression, "I have had it," means that whatever we have had, it holds no promise for the future. The despair of life is to realize that our treasures have no meaning for the future.

Robert Townsend, in his best seller, *Up the Organization* (Knopf 1970), says this about our modern approach to work. "And look at the rewards we are offering our people today: higher wages, medical benefits, vacations, pensions, profit sharing, bowling and baseball teams. *Not one can be enjoyed on the job.* You've got to leave work, get sick, or retire first. No wonder people aren't having fun on the job." Jesus had this kind of living in mind when he said, "You have had your time of happiness." It is a great thing to be a part of something whose word is not only of what has gone before but "Behold, I make all things new."

WHAT'S INSIDE?

> "A good man produces good from the store of good within himself; and an evil man from evil within produces evil. For the words that the mouth utters come from the overflowing of the heart."   6:45

Albertus Magnus, a great teacher, became curious about a young man named Thomas Aquinas. He called Aquinas into his study and asked him a few questions. He got his opinions about theology and discussed with him grammar and logic. When he spoke to the crowded assembly the next time, his word was,

"You call our brother Thomas a dumb ox, do you? I tell you that some day the whole world will listen to his bellowing" (*Living Biographies of Great Philosophers,* by Thomas and Thomas, Doubleday, 1959). What the listeners had called dumbness in this quiet young man, the great teacher had seen as deep qualities of goodness and commitment. What we have within comes out, and this is why we can never pretend to be something we are not for very long. Our lives are a building up and a conserving. The crisis does not suddenly change us. What we have stored within us through our actions and our attitudes becomes the goodness or the evil manifest in the hour of danger. I remember in the city where I lived a man was under fire from the far right. A newspaper editor said to me, "Can they not see that here is a good man?" Unless we are blinded by some prejudice, the goodness or the evil deep within a man becomes apparent to us.

RELIGION AS A GAME

"We piped for you and you would not dance."
"We wept and wailed, and you would not mourn."   7:32

Jesus said that his generation were like children playing in the marketplace, complaining because their companions would not respond to their mood. If they were playing "funerals" their companions were not in the mood to mourn, and if they changed the game to "weddings" they were not ready to rejoice. Religion to you, said Jesus, is just a game you play. He would say the same thing to us, for this generation has come to regard its religion as merely a game.

This means that we think the purpose of the church, of preaching, and of the Christian faith is to please our mood. We do not want to be upset or disturbed with ideas contrary to the general pattern we have accepted. When the late John Steinbeck wrote that delightful book, *Travels with Charlie*, he commented on hearing a man preach in a small New England church on a Sunday morning. The sermon, Steinbeck says, told him and the congregation that they were no good and it was only the mercy of God that prevented their destruction. The author makes something of this because he was not in the habit of hearing it and he thought it a great and healing experience to hear a preacher speak in those harsh tones. But for the most part, we expect our ministers to preach what we want to hear.

Thomas Carlyle, in *Sartor Resartus*, said, "To me also was given, if not victory, yet the consciousness of battle, and the resolve to persevere therein while life or faculty is left." This is the spirit we must have when we join the church, not the easy-going attitude which will respond only to the mood we happen to be in at that particular time.

ACCORDING TO OUR EXPERIENCE

> "And so, I tell you, her great love proves that her many sins have been forgiven; where little has been forgiven, little love is shown."   7:47

The gap between the generations is not a difference in age, but a difference in experience. The young cannot be expected to respond the same way as their elders: they have never been through the searing times their fathers have known. Jesus says that love is a part of that same principle. This woman knew what it was to have her sins forgiven and the love of her life was based on that experience.

It is the testimony of these saints who have been forgiven so much that influences the world. R. W. Randall, a Victorian preacher, said that as he grew older he never ceased to marvel at the deep religion he saw in the life of the English peasant. He said that sometimes when he was giving them communion, he wanted to kneel down and kiss their hands. Simon, the Pharisee, could not see this until Jesus said that though forgiveness is a free gift, it is hard for a man to accept.

THE WOMEN

> These women provided for them out of their own resources.   8:3

The Christian faith honored women and changed their status. They had been thought of as chattels, but Christians thought of them as the daughters of God. Jesus found that for him and his disciples, women made provision. The raising of the status of womanhood was not the least of Christianity's contributions to society.

Once when John Wesley was preaching, a drunken priest of the Church of England started to shout and cause trouble. All that his *Journal* says about it is that a few resolute women took the man by the arm and sent him on his way. It has been these "resolute women" who have meant so much to Christianity.

Noel Coward had profound admiration for Marie Tempest, and he welcomed every chance to work with her. This is what he said about her: "She has more allure and glamor and charm at seventy than most women I know who are in their twenties and thirties. Her dignity is unassailable and I have a strong feeling that it always was; I think what impresses me most about her is her unspoken but very definite demand for good behavior." (*Talent to Amuse,* by Morley, Doubleday, 1969). Said the early pagan world, "What women these Christians have!"

GROW UP!

> ". . . . but their further growth is choked by cares and
> wealth and the pleasures of life, and they bring
> nothing to maturity."   8:14

Halford Luccock called these three "a trinity of suffocation."
One of these suffocators is "cares." Nearly everybody has at least
one care in his life. If we could be set free from useless anxiety
and constant worry, our life would be a constant development to
the end. The second suffocator is wealth, which does not mean
that we must actually possess it to fall its victim. If we desire
it more than we should, it will cut us off with domination of our
minds. The third suffocator is pleasure when it becomes a final
goal.

Jesus says that such people bring nothing to maturity. The
saddest people in the world are those who never realize their
potential. I meet them in the ministry and I am shocked. This
man promised so much at one time and has turned out to be
immature. Something choked off his growth. Or another showed
great promise in youth, but it gave way to bitterness and com-
plaint. Possibilities—but nothing matured. The psychologists are
right in stressing maturity. We are to grow into the mature
status of the sons of God, and whatever suffocates this urge is
tragedy. Remember Robert Louis Stevenson's lines, in *Looking
Forward:*

> When I am grown to man's estate
> I shall be very proud and great,
> And tell the other girls and boys
> Not to meddle with my toys.

I AM SUNK!

> They went to him, and roused him, crying, "Master Master, we are sinking!" 8:24

Robert Burton wrote: "The winds are mad, they know not whence they come, nor whither they would go: and those men are maddest of all who go to sea." But life is a journey which we all have to undertake, and an ocean voyage, with all its perils, is one of the best descriptions of it. We forget that there is much more water on our planet than there is land. We must learn to sail on, between the threat of destruction and the danger of sinking. The disciples learned this fundamental lesson on the lake. Read the 107th Psalm:

> Others there are who go to sea in ships
> and make their living on the wide waters.
> These men have seen the acts of the Lord
> and his marvellous doings in the deep.
> At his command the storm-wind rose
> and lifted the waves high.
> Carried up to heaven, plunged down to the depths,
> tossed to and fro in peril,
> they reeled and staggered like drunken men,
> and their seamanship was all in vain.
> So they cried to the Lord in their trouble,
> and he brought them out of their distress. (23–28)

FEAR

> Then the whole population of the Gergesene district asked him to go, for they were in the grip of a great fear. 8:37

Jesus healed a man of what they called an "unclean spirit." That spirit had gone out of the man and into the swine, which had gone over the cliff into the lake and were drowned. At once the people urged Jesus to leave their part of the country, "for they were in the grip of a great fear." Jesus sometimes made people afraid, and life is full of fears.

Edward Gibbon, writing in the eighteenth century about his own school experiences, said, "A school is a cavern of fear and sorrow: the mobility of the captive youths is chained to a book and a desk: an inflexible master commands their attention, which, every moment, is impatient to escape: they labor, like the soldiers in Persia, under the scourge: and their education is nearly finished before they can apprehend the sense or utility of the harsh lessons, which they are forced to repeat" (Gibbon, *Memoirs of My Life,* edited by Bonnard, 1966).

Suspicion haunts our minds and blinds us to goodness. Most of the harm in the world is done by men who are scared. One of the great works which Jesus performs is to set men free from the "grip of a great fear."

History is full of tragic stories of nations plunging into war because of their fear, when a little time and a little discussion might have prevented it. W. H. Maltby once said, "In the Sermon on the Mount, Jesus promised his disciples three things —that they would be entirely fearless, absurdly happy, and that they would get into trouble. They did get into trouble, and found to their surprise that they were not afraid. They were absurdly happy, for they laughed over their own troubles and only cried over other people's."

SOMETHING BEYOND US

> Now Prince Herod heard of all that was happening, and did not know what to make of it. . . .   9:7

Herod heard all the wonderful things about Jesus' ministry and could not tell what it meant. People say about the Christian gospel that it is all a mystery and they do "not know what to make of it."

A skeptical young man said to the preacher, "I do not want to offend you but I really believe that all that you have been saying is moonshine." To which the preacher replied, "That is a very good comparison, my boy. It is moonshine that moves the tides of the ocean, and what looks so ephemeral is the mighty force that moves billions of tons of water. By the way," he added, "have you ever stood at a place such as the Bay of Fundy and watched the tide come in? Next time you see that sight, think of religion."

William James wrote, "I am against bigness and greatness in all their forms, and with the invisible molecular moral forces at work from individual to individual, stealing in through all the crannies of the world like so many soft rootlets, or like the capillary oozing of water, and yet rending the hardest moments of man's pride, if you give them time." Herod faced something he could not understand because it was neither military nor obviously mighty.

WIDER THAN OUR MINDS

> "Do not stop him, for he who is not against you is on
> your side."   9:50

The ecumenical movement has taught us that there is more to hold us together than there is to drive us apart. We have allowed differences to become too big, and we have failed to see the many on our side. The ecumenical movement has taught us that no church has all the truth and every church has something we ought to learn about rather than fight against.

In every community there are people who are not articulate but whose hearts are with the Christians. One of the best things the church can learn is not to spend time attacking its friends but learn to recognize them. It is time for us to rise and sing together the hymn: "There's a wideness in God's mercy, like the wideness of the sea."

DON'T LOOK BACK

> "No one who sets his hand to the plough and then
> keeps looking back is fit for the kingdom of God."
> 9:62

The older generation cannot forget "the good old days," which are not as good as they remember.

The church falls into this trap more easily than most institutions because the church deals with eternity. When a churchman talks about the days of big revivals or of class meetings as if these were the great Christian witnesses he must hold to, he is like the plowman more interested in seeing where he has come from than where he is going.

In *Ben-Gurion: The Armed Prophet,* Bar-Zohr writes: "Ben-Gurion won because he is a 'searchlight that beams all his power on a single point, leaving everything else in obscurity.'" It is this concentration of attention and energy that achieves. Looking back usually weakens our dedication. Remember the wise words of Satchel Paige: "Don't look back. Somebody might be gainin' on you."

Jesus' concern was that his disciples keep their eyes on the future. We are directed toward tomorrow. To follow God is to believe in the road ahead and the great things which wait for us around the next bend. We may sing about "the old-time religion," but if we understand it, we will know that Christianity is a spur and a promise. There is nothing quite so much at home in a revolutionary time as the gospel of Jesus Christ.

CHOOSE THE BEST

> "The part that Mary has chosen is best. . . ."   10:42

I have sympathy for Martha, as I have sympathy for the elder brother of the Prodigal Son. When one is making the practical and hard arrangements for the dinner, it is most annoying to see someone else following more "spiritual" pursuits and giving no help. But the lesson here is plain enough.

Life is a feast, but we cannot eat everything. Life is choice, and we must decide what comes first. If we take one thing, we cannot take the other. So the Lord says to Martha, "You are fretting and fussing about so many things." An apt description of our generation and of us who are so busy.

I learned something about this some years ago in a political campaign. The old pro told us not to scatter our shots everywhere but to decide on a few key places we must win and concentrate our energy there.

I think of the ministry, where a man does not punch a time clock and no one sets his schedule. The problem for us is finding what comes first. There are not many lazy men in the ministry, but there are many ministers whose energies are scattered.

BE SHAMELESS!

> "I tell you that even if he will not provide for him out of friendship, the very shamelessness of the request will make him get up and give him all he needs."
>
> 11:8

I think of men like Stanley Jones and Frank Laubach, who had such great projects depending upon them and who shared them with every man they met. There was a kind of shamelessness about them that had power.

Jesus tells us that God likes the kind of people who ask for great things. We do not ask for enough. We forget that we are coming to a King whose resources are wider than the world.

If we believe in our cause, that is a cure for our bashfulness. Because it is something beyond ourselves we have a carefree shamelessness. Said William James: "The greatest use of life is to spend it for something that will outlast it."

One of my long-time friends was the secretary of a church board of evangelism. He never missed an opportunity to tell someone about Christ. If he got into an elevator with one other person, he would be telling him about Christ before they got to the second floor. He was shameless.

CLEANSING THE CUP

> **"But let what is in the cup be given in charity, and all is clean."**　　　　　　　　　　　　　　　　　　11:41

The Pharisees clean the outside of the cup but leave the inside filled with greed and wickedness. How shall it be made clean? Jesus said that giving what is in the cup in charity cleansed it all.

Samuel Coleridge said, "The happiness of life is made up of minute fractions; the little soon-forgotten charities of a kiss or a smile, a kind look, a heartfelt compliment, countless infinitesimals of pleasurable and congenial feelings." To give ourselves in charity is to clean the gift which we present.

The organized charity by which our society takes care of its poor and unfortunate turns easily into something cold and mechanical. John Boyle O'Reilly wrote:

> The organized charity, scrimped and iced,
> In the name of a cautious, statistical Christ.
>
> (In Bohemian)

But in the verse from Luke, Jesus is speaking of the spontaneous act springing from the kind heart.

Mark Twain said, in *Pudd'nhead Wilson's Calendar:* "Remember the poor—it costs nothing." And that is precisely what such concern is worth. But when given in charity, it transforms both the recipient and the giver, so it is hard to tell which was most blessed.

HOW IT IS WITH THE RICH

> "That is how it is with the man who amasses wealth
> for himself and remains a pauper in the sight of
> God." 12:21

The story of The Rich Fool ends with this text. The gospel contrasts wealthy men and their poverty of spirit. They are paupers in the sight of God.

In British history, Francis Bacon is an example of the poverty of the rich. Brilliant, cynical, and able, he was appointed lord keeper to King James in 1617. Then in 1621 he became lord chancellor. But in that same year the House of Commons brought charges against him for taking bribes. In spite of his brilliance his whole life came crashing down. Rich in so many things, he was a pauper. Logan Pearsall Smith wrote, in *Afterthoughts,* "It is the wretchedness of being rich that you have to live with rich people."

An old preacher who had an amazing influence but was not a gifted speaker was explained by one who knew him: "There are twenty years of holy living behind every sermon." Know the people who have ignored wealth for themselves so that they can be rich toward God. These are the heroes of the gospel.

BUT YOU HAVE A FATHER

> "For all these are things for the heathen to run after;
> but you have a Father who knows that you need
> them." 12:30

If you are seeking the calm and quiet of the Christian faith and ask where it comes from and why it is, this word explains it. When we believe, "but you have a Father," our lives are filled with quietness and confidence. Theodore Parker said, "Every rose is an autograph from the hand of God on His world about us." These autographs are all about us testifying to the presence of One whom our Lord said we should address as our Father. Men live in the consciousness of this truth, and, like George Washington Carver, carve over their workplaces, "God's little workshop."

ACTION

> **"Be ready for action, with belts fastened and lamps alight."** 12:35

What is the pose of a Christian man? He should be in prayer or in meditation. But Jesus says he must be ready for action with lamps burning. His word will strike a responsive note with the young. Jesus would have liked the rebellious generation which has made up its mind to challenge the status quo.

The football players at Columbia University signed a petition to support a students' war protest strike. Bob Hacket, one of the players, explained the action in these words: "It is an attempt to dispel President Nixon's image that athletes are all part of the famous 'silent majority.' I am a moderate, I believe in the system, and I am putting my faith in Congress, but I wouldn't mind helping a peace candidate this summer. I have never done anything like that before, but I think it is time for people to stop sitting on their rears." The words are Hacket's, but the spirit is from Jesus.

Winston Churchill in one of his cynical and critical moods, in which he was not always fair, said, "Look at the Swiss! They have enjoyed peace for centuries. What do they produce? The cuckoo clock!" Life is struggle and danger, and there was never one who faced it more courageously than our Lord. The church is wrong when it appeals only to those who prefer ease at any price and neglects the young and the adventurous.

A POUND OF RESPONSIBILITY
FOR AN OUNCE OF HONOR

> ". . . and the more a man has had entrusted to him the
> more he will be required to repay."   12:48

Presiding over the election of a Methodist bishop in Europe in
the fall of 1970, I said to the man who had been elected, "You
will find that the old maxim is true: for every ounce of honor
you receive there will be a pound of responsibility." It is a law
of life—to whom much has been given, much shall be required.

The Reformation heritage is an extra responsibility upon individual Christians. It is easier and safer to turn decisions and
responsibility over to a hierarchy. Some of the weird results
which have come out of the freedom of Protestant churches
indicate that for some responsibility is too heavy a burden to
bear.

Democracy is a way of life which is rooted in Thomas Jeffer-
son's remark that "one man with courage is a majority." Our
faith is that if he is right, he will win over the majority. The
question is always whether people are decent enough or wise
enough to govern themselves. If we are to be free, we will have
to pay the price for it.

Jesus said that when we have been given strength, we must
use it as a service to God. Pay for it we must, if we are to keep
it. Keir Hardie, a political leader with a deep religious sense,
was angered in 1897 when he thought of the Christians taking
Christ's name in vain and not being able to "see his image
being crucified in every hungry child." "We have no right to a
merry Christmas so many of our fellows cannot share," he said.
This word of our Lord comes not as comfort, but as a scourge.

IF WE LET HIM

> "How often have I longed to gather your children, as
> a hen gathers her brood under her wings; but you
> would not let me."   13:34

There is an incident in Morris West's novel, *The Shoes of the Fisherman*. The Pope, after his coronation, walks through the streets of Rome. He comes to a poor apartment house where a man is dying. The family have waited too long, and there is no hope for the man. The Pope, however, wants to help the family, but the young woman who has been nursing the dying man says, "They can cope with death. It is only living that defeats them." We prefer death to letting Jesus bring us life.

LET'S GIVE A PARTY

> "But when you give a party, ask the poor, the crippled,
> the lame, and the blind; and so find happiness."
>   14:13

When I saw "Hello Dolly," I left saying to myself, "This is what going to church ought to be." I left with a song ringing in my heart and feeling good about life. That does not happen often in church services.

This word of Jesus to his followers urges us to give a party for the kind of people most hosts would not invite. It ends with the promise, "and so find happiness." This is indeed a different and radical insight into the nature of the Christian life. It ought to have something of the nature of a party ending with happiness. Worship is celebration.

The reason people become impatient with the church is that it lacks sparkle. They seek a new form of worship that will restore the hope and promise they remember as young people. Christians are to give a party for those who cannot repay them. The result is happiness. Try it!

I read letters from young men and young women who have been with the Peace Corps. After describing what they do, essentially what Jesus commanded us to do, they tell me about a fresh look at the church. They found something the gospel has been telling them about but which they have discovered in reality. It is shocking that a government-sponsored project gives them what the church ought to be giving to its members every day.

FULL HOUSE

"I want my house to be full."   14:23

Nothing is more discouraging than to give a dinner and have it poorly attended. I am not fond of crowds and can find excuses for not going to meetings, but on Sunday morning at the time of the church service, I must confess that I am like the man who said, "I want my house to be full." It does not have to be a big church, for I find as much satisfaction in preaching in a small one if it is full. The failure of the Christian church is the empty pew at the worship service.

I listen to talk about "small groups," and I realize that they have their place and that some things can be done only through them. But this kind of talk from men who are making excuses for not appealing to all kinds of conditions of men is not fooling anyone. After all the excuses are made, the truth is that a half-empty church is a witness to lifelessness in the congregation and inadequacy in the pulpit.

It is a good thing for us to be critical of ourselves and of our world. It is not a good thing for us to take these criticisms as excuses for half-empty churches. It is still true that if there is something vital, something essential to life, people will get there and hear about it. When Jesus Christ puts on a dinner it will be worth attending and the house will be full.

HOW MUCH WILL IT COST?

> "Would any of you think of building a tower without
> first sitting down and calculating the cost, to see
> whether he could afford to finish it?"   14:28

Jesus counsels us to be careless about the risks involved. But
here is a command to calculate the cost to see if we can afford it.
Which is to say that life is full of paradox. To make it a purely
logical proposition is not possible. Of course, we have to consider the cost, and certainly we have to consider the worth.

Accepting the gospel is a costly affair. First of all we must
make a commitment to something we must have, no matter
how much we must sacrifice for it. Two of the main questions
we have to ask are: first, what can I afford? And second, what
must I have no matter what it costs? Thoreau dealt with this
issue in a simple observation: "All good things are cheap; all
bad are very dear" (*Journal,* March 3, 1841).

REJOICE!

> " 'Rejoice with me!' he cries. 'I have found my lost
> sheep.' "   15:6

Every man knows something about losing something valuable
and finding it. He must tell his friends about it that they may
rejoice with him. This is the way it is with God over one sinner
who repents and comes home.

Begin with the assumption that there is a right path and that
it is very easy to miss it. Someone pointed out that sheep "nibble
themselves lost." They just begin to follow what they think is
the greenest grass and before they know it they have separated
themselves from the flock and hidden themselves from the
shepherd. The world is an easy place to get lost. The prevailing
sickness of our time is not rebellion, but lostness. We are aware

of that searching Presence that follows us until He finds us. This is what the gospel is really about. Under its guiding word we find the straight path.

STAMP OUT BOREDOM

" 'Then he came to his senses. . . .' "   15:17

I have listened to men tell me their problems, and I have said to myself that to get into such a mess they must have been out of their minds. The lawyer who decides to let his client plead "temporary insanity" is simply looking realistically at things which human beings do to themselves and others, and the plea is logical.

What causes this behavior? Often it is caused by boredom. We are enslaved by the routine and it drives us mad. We want to break loose and go to a far country; find new friends; live. Thomas Hoving, the Director of the Metropolitan Museum of Art in New York City, said: "One thing I would like to see ... instead of one of those wonderful plaques they usually mount on a school—God knows where they get most of their quotes— would be a big plaque mounted on the entrance to proclaim boldly: 'This school is dedicated to stamping out boredom.' " I would like to see such a plaque on every church. Think of the gospel as a way of life which will "stamp out boredom."

THIS HAPPY DAY

> " 'How could we help celebrating this happy day?' "
>
> 15:32

This is the word of the father to the older brother who has been sulking because of his own lack of recognition. How can we help celebrating? is a good question for the Christian church to ask.

There is more rejoicing among the people of faith than among those who are merely studying the whole business. If you are ever at a meeting with people of Christian conviction, you will notice that the songs they sing all reflect joy and a sense of victory. The old revival hymns all have this note. While I would not want to argue that the "good" music of the more sophisticated congregation is not pleasing to the Lord, I would suggest that people more concerned with good taste and seeing things done in proper order also have a tendency to have less fun in their religion. A Salvation Army man was making too much noise on the drums for the taste of the director. He apologized and said, "I will try to make less noise, but when I think what the Lord has done for me, I want to bust the bloomin' drum." A congregation ought to sing at least once a year:

> O Happy Day, that fixed my choice
> On thee my savior and my God.

Jesus says that the greatest joy of all is celebrating the return of a lost son to God's family. The angels in heaven participate, and when, unlike the older brother, we rejoice too, we have built a bridge from time to eternity.

DIVIDING LINE

> "Until John, it was the Law and the prophets: since then, there is the good news of the kingdom of God...."   16:16

Here is the dividing line in men's knowledge of the way God deals with them. The good news of the kingdom of God is something different from anything before, and this break is something that Christians must understand.

The Resurrection is the dividing line. On which side of it do we live? And on which side of it do we make our ultimate decisions? This is conversion, and the new man in Christ knows that something decisive has taken place which changes everything that he thinks and does. In one of Robert Louis Stevenson's stories, "The Ebb Tide," one of the characters cries out, "Everything's grace. We walk upon it, we breathe it, we live and die by it, it makes the nails and axles of the universe!" That is the Christian's life when he has moved forward from the Law and the prophets to hear "the good news of the kingdom of God."

Thomas Carlyle wrote in an essay in 1832, soon after the death of his father: "He was religious with the consent of his whole faculties. Without religion he would have been nothing. Indeed, his habit of intellect was thoroughly free, and even incredulous. And strangely enough did the daily example of this work afterwards on me.... Religion was the pole-star for my father. Rude and uncultivated as he otherwise was, it made him and kept him 'in all points a man.'" He heard the good news of the kingdom of God.

HEALING ON THE WAY

> ...and while they were on their way, they were
> made clean.   17:14

The main point of the story is that Jesus healed ten lepers, but
only one was grateful and returned to thank his healer. But this
particular phrase in the story opens up a great truth of life and
the good news. The lepers were not healed immediately; they
were healed gradually, "while they were on their way."

We want the whole promise fulfilled immediately. A man
said to me one time, "If I had faith like yours, I would be a
Christian." I had to say to him that faith is not given at the
beginning. We find faith while we are on the way.

All that we are promised is light enough for the next step.
The whole is not revealed to us, and the mystery of life never becomes clear at the beginning. But we will be shown what we
ought to do immediately and what the next decision ought to
be. That is enough for us, and it is all we have a right to expect.

The truth is that a miracle waits at the end of the road, and
the best is yet to be. In the meantime, many good things come
to us, if we are on our way. A friend reported that he saw on
the wall of a hospital chaplain's office, a plaque with these
words: "The sign of God is that we shall be led in a way we
had not planned to go." But planned or not, He heals us when
we are on the way.

BE A NUISANCE

> " '. . . but this widow is so great a nuisance that I will
> see her righted before she wears me out with her
> persistence.' "   18:5

The world owes much to nuisances. More progress has been
made because somebody made a nuisance of himself than we

realize. Most social progress had at its center a man or a woman who had mastered the fine art of being a nuisance.

When Wendell Phillips was going out to one of the endless meetings where, as usual, he intended to speak against slavery, the parting words of his wife were, "Now, Wendell, don't you shilly-shally." She was saying that he must never give up being a nuisance and become a man who pleased everybody. The Abolitionist Movement was made victorious finally by the nuisances it was able to enlist.

The prophets of the Old Testament were nuisances. They bothered the king, annoyed the well-to-do, disturbed the comfortable. But their continuing persistence got action. The church at its best always produces nuisances.

Some we call muckrakers and some we call reformers. But they are the people who finally push society forward. They are the men who are not afraid of making nuisances of themselves. They know that society is like that judge who may not act out of any burning desire for justice but will often do right for the sake of quiet.

YOU AIN'T SEEN NOTHING YET

> ... and they thought the reign of God might dawn
> at any moment.   19:11

This is the meaning of the Incarnation. Being in the presence of Jesus makes us believe that God's kingdom is about to be realized. We have seen it already in him.

Those who believe that the Christian faith is always looking backward had better read the gospels again. It has this constant sense of expectancy which makes the present exciting. That something great is about to happen is the way Christians felt and they never could give in to despair or surrender to boredom.

This is what a great book, or a great painting, or a great experience does for people. Billy Wilder, commenting on his philosophy of making motion pictures, said, "I am not going to reform the audience. I am not going to better the audience. I just want the audience to drop the popcorn and listen" (Wood, *The Bright Side of Billy Wilder, Primarily,* Doubleday, 1969). The experience of making people forget their popcorn and listen characterizes the gospel. Yesterday was full of great experiences, but we have not seen anything yet. As the cabby explained the inscription: "What is Past is Prologue" on a public monument in Washington, D.C.: "Mac, that's just government talk for 'You ain't seen nothing yet.'" A truly Christian sentiment.

GOD'S MOMENTS

> "... because you did not recognize God's moment
> when it came."   19:44

God's moments are often not recognized until after the event is past. It was in the moment when our eyes were opened to a new truth that our lives were changed. It was the moment when the girl we proposed to said yes. It was the moment when a vision came into our minds of what we wanted to do and what we wanted to be. It was the moment we made a decision to take this turn and not that one.

For nations, it is a decisive battle such as Waterloo, which Victor Hugo described as a time when God decided that he had enough of Napoleon. It may be for America the time when we decide that freedom does not lie on the road of pornography and that we are through with such military adventures as Vietnam.

CHRISTIAN OPPORTUNITY

> "You will be brought before synagogues and put in
> prison; you will be haled before kings and governors
> for your allegiance to me. This will be your oppor-
> tunity to testify. . . ."   21:12-13

Henry James told George Bernard Shaw that he had heard it
was not unusual for Shaw to speak in parks before groups who
gathered around to hear his ideas about socialism and life. Shaw
confessed this was true and that on one occasion he had had over
a hundred people around him as he harangued them on his fav-
orite subject. Henry James shook his head in wonderment and
said, "I never could do that." Well, the early Christians could
do it, and without an organization of paid clergy they spread
the good news. Paul did it, and he had some of his most fruitful
encounters in prison. For the Christian, every occasion, good or
bad, is a chance to bear witness.

The Methodist movement began when John Wesley over-
came his high church prejudices and brought himself to proclaim the good news in the open air before the common people.
He began preaching the gospel to the people on Haddam
Mount, outside Bristol, and he wrote in his *Journal* for March
31, 1739: ". . . having been all my life (till very lately) so
tenacious of every point relating to decency and order, that I
should have thought the saving of souls almost a sin, if it had
not been done in a church." When he went out to preach on
the afternoon of April 2, 1739, he noted in his *Journal:* "At
four in the afternoon, I submitted to be more vile, and proclaimed in the highways the glad tidings of salvation, speaking
from a little eminence in a ground adjoining to the city, to about
three thousand people." Such was his feeling about field-preach-
ing, but it was opportunity, and his ministry had amazing results.

Preaching is primarily testifying. We ought not to be too personal in what we say; people get tired of constant references to our families. What the man in the pew wants to know is simply an answer to the question—what has the gospel done for you in your situation? If we can tell him this simply, we will be helping him.

I let a man come in ahead of me from an access road onto a busy freeway one day. I heard him speak at a meeting later on and refer to this simple act as "Christianity on the freeway." I wish I were always polite, but he happened to catch me at just the right moment. We are always testifying to something, and blessed is the man whose testimony is of what the Lord has done for him.

DON'T GET TRAPPED

> "Keep a watch on yourselves; do not let your minds be dulled by dissipation and drunkenness and wordly cares so that the great Day closes upon you suddenly like a trap. . . ."   21:34

Examination day in school may be something to welcome, but it may also be something to fear. As a little notice on the bulletin board of a high school in Florida put it, "As long as there are examinations there will be prayers in schools."

Great days come to us all, and if we are ready for them they are days of opportunity. But for the man who has sinned against time, the day is the closing of a trap from which there is no escape. Judgment can be either the happiest or the most miserable of days.

SHARE IT AMONG YOURSELVES

> **Then he took a cup, and after giving thanks he said,
> "Take this and share it among yourselves. . . ."**
>
> 22:17

Here is a meaning of the communion seldom emphasized. This
has nothing to do with remembering Jesus, but simply with his
command that we share the wine with each other. The Last
Supper was not only a symbol of relationship between the disciples and Christ, it was also a symbol of their constant duty to
one another. They were to share.

Older Christians are shocked by some of the informal communion services now being observed. It may be that by thus
making them informal we are getting closer to their original
meaning. A Sunday School class of young slum children were
acting out "The Last Supper." The teacher was somewhat
startled when the little boy acting the part of Jesus said, "Well,
fellas, I ain't going to be with you much longer." That is hardly
more shocking than Jesus' words, "Take this and share it."

THOSE WHO STAND BY

> **"You are the men who have stood firmly by me in my
> times of trial. . . ."**
>
> 22:28

So Jesus addressed his disciples at the Last Supper. One of them
did betray him, and others ran away, and yet these were the
men who had been through the hard experiences and they were
still with him.

When a man looks back over his ministry, he remembers
those men who were with him through his trials. There are the
laymen who helped him when he was discouraged and whose
faithfulness was in itself a source of inspiration. This is the
relationship between beloved members of a congregation and
the pastor.

This is a description of the church. We have our share of fair-weather followers who stay as long as they are pleased and who leave when the going gets rough. But the church is a fellowship of those people "who have stood firmly." Religion has never been to them their immediate feelings. It has been a matter of commitment and of enlistment. Religion is a commitment of one's life to a cause.

Lloyd Douglas told of one of his parishioners who was an old music teacher. Asked one day what was the good word, the teacher struck a tuning fork hanging on a cord, and he said, "That is the good word. That is G and no matter how the weather may change or what may happen to human affairs it remains G." Jesus was saying that to his disciples. The rewards of the kingdom would go finally to those "who have stood firmly by me in my times of trial."

HOURS OF DARKNESS

> "But this is your moment—the hour when darkness reigns." 22:53

Jesus' word to those who have arrested him and plot his execution has this quiet, calm note. It is their hour and, for the time being, darkness reigns. How different is our own reaction when things go wrong and the prophets of our time proclaim that we are at the end of the Christian era and facing the beginning of something which is a complete denial of our faith. His word is that these hours of darkness are on the same level as the hours of assured victory. They are all a part of life and they are all under God's ultimate rule.

A picture which was taken during World War II shows some Jewish people being driven from the Warsaw ghetto by Nazi soldiers. Down in the front is a little boy with his hands up and a look of uncertainty and fear on his face. A Nazi soldier is standing behind him, with his gun pointed at the boy. The youngster seems to be saying, "What kind of a world is this and what are you doing to me now? What have I done?" The soldier who held that gun was caught and sentenced as a war criminal. That hour was one of darkness indeed for the Jewish people.

God has not ordained that we should follow a constant path of progress. There are times when the enemy rises and threatens all the good we have tried to accomplish. That is a time when we need the spirit of Christ, which simply accepts those hours of darkness with the underlying certainty that they are not final.

DECISIONS BY SHOUTING

Their shouts prevailed and Pilate decided that they should have their way.   23:24

At a noisy election rally in the South, a speaker stood up and urged the people to consider the issues at stake and then decide on the men they would support. "Think," he said, "Think." One man shouted back from the crowd, "We didn't come here to think. We came here to holler." It happens that way in some elections.

I am impressed by how much noise a few people can make when they are bent upon shouting down the opposition. Many times in a meeting we listen to the speeches and decide that the vote is going to be very close. Then the vote is taken and it is overwhelming on one side, with only a few on the other. But each one of those few had made a speech.

THE BURNING HEART

> "Did we not feel our hearts on fire as he talked with
> us on the road and explained the scriptures to us?"
>
> 24:32

Here is the word of one of the travelers thinking of the effect
the Stranger had on them on the way to Emmaus. The presence
of Jesus, he was saying, can always be recognized when one's
heart feels as if it were on fire.

One of John Wesley's biographers entitled his book simply,
Knight of the Burning Heart. It is a good title for the biography
of a man whose effectiveness began when his heart was strangely
warmed. Every man who has moved people and affected great
accomplishments has had this power of making hearts catch fire.

A quotation I value greatly is entitled "One Solitary Life."
"He was born in an obscure village, the child of a peasant
woman. He grew up in still another village, where he worked
in a carpenter shop until he was thirty. Then for three years he
was an itinerant preacher. He never wrote a book. He never
held an office. He never had a family or owned a house. He
didn't go to college. He never visited a big city. He never
traveled two hundred miles from the place where he was born.
He did none of the things one usually associates with greatness.
He had no credentials but himself. He was only thirty-three
when the tide of public opinion turned against him. His friends
ran away. He was turned over to his enemies and went through
the mockery of a trial. He was nailed to a cross between two
thieves. While he was dying, his executioners gambled for his
clothing, the only property he had on earth. When he was
dead, he was laid in a borrowed grave through the pity of a
friend. Nineteen centuries have come and gone, and today he is
the central figure of the human race and the leader of mankind's
progress. I am well within the mark when I say that all the
armies that ever marched, all the navies that ever sailed, all the
parliaments that ever sat, all the kings that ever reigned, put

together, have not affected the life of man on this earth as much as that one solitary life." His power to make men's hearts burn within them is one of the sure signs of His divinity.

YOU SAW IT HAPPEN

> "Begin from Jerusalem; it is you who are the witnesses
> to it all."   24:48

Ministers have often inisisted that the gospel was a thing of the country rather than the city, but Christianity began at Jeruslem and St. Paul preached it in the great urban centers of his time. Paul died at Rome, and the witness of his imprisonment there is one of the most fruitful of early Christianity. Jesus' word to his disciples was to begin where they were and to remember that they were witnesses to the fulfillment of the gospel.

Men who had been through what the disciples had been through had a whole new point of view regarding God, man and the world. Ignazio Silone, the Italian writer, said: "To oppose Fascism, we need neither heavy armaments nor bureaucratic apparatuses. What we need above all is a different way of looking at life and human beings. My dear friends, without this different way of looking at life and human beings, we shall ourselves become Fascists." Christians are those who have "a different way of looking at life and human beings." On this foundation the Christian church rests.

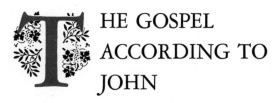

THE GOSPEL ACCORDING TO JOHN

INTRODUCTION

> So the Word became flesh; he came to dwell among
> us, and we saw his glory, such glory as befits the
> Father's only Son, full of grace and truth.   1:14

St. John's gospel differs markedly from the other three gospels.
It is often referred to as "The Fourth Gospel," to set it apart.
Someone once said that the first three gospels represent the news
columns of the paper, but the Fourth Gospel is the editoral
page. John is concerned more with the meanings of "life in
Christ," and he sees the events in Palestine as opening up
grand truths about God and the universe.

John's gospel was written around A.D. 100. The traditional
view assumed the author to be the son of Zebedee, the apostle.
It is possible that the beginnings of the gospel are rooted in that
disciple's memoirs and comments. Another tradition holds that
the author might have been "the beloved disciple." Whoever
the author was, he was someone with a special relationship to
Jesus Christ, who was utterly convinced of the eternal significance of the life of Christ for men. We know that in the first
century there lived a man called John the Elder, who was much
respected and loved. He had a place of prominence in the
church, and perhaps he put some finishing touches on this
gospel.

A chief impression of the Gospel of John in the New English
Bible is that the book could have easily become so "spiritual"
as to ignore the earthly life of a Galilean man of the first

century. Yet it is nothing of the kind, because it is rooted in history. It never forgets that Jesus was a man who lived in a particular time and in a particular place. This historical sense makes it a gospel indeed, and saves it from being merely a speculative writing. It begins with the marvelous Logos doctrine, but it never can escape the conviction, "so the Word became flesh." It is the story of the Incarnation.

To begin with, it is a picture of revelation. How does a man find God? We are likely to regard it as a hard job, demanding all of a man's dedication and devotion. To most of us, religion is the act of seeking until we find.

But this gospel, even as the Bible as a whole, contains a great surprise. It says our search is from the wrong end, and that its truth comes by revelation. We do not seek God so much as God seeks us, and when we say that we have found God, it really means that to some extent He has already found us. Revelation comes from One who is more anxious to reveal Himself than we are to seek Him. God takes the initiative: that is the good news of John.

A man wrote to Albert Einstein and asked him to describe the theory of relativity in simple words, so that he might at least catch a glimpse of the meaning. Einstein answered that he could not do what the man requested, but if he would call on him at Princeton, Einstein could play it on his violin. God replied to man's hunger for a glimpse of God by his revelation in Jesus Christ.

John's gospel also says that God reveals eternal life in the commonplace. Remember this when thinking about the church. It is full of weakness and it makes mistakes, but it has eternal significance. Within this fellowship the eternal breaks into the ordinary affairs of our lives. The church made up of men and women, rich and poor, bright and dull, young people with their dreams and their hopes, little children with their orneriness and their angelic qualities. And all reveal God, who finds us in daily and sometimes tiring events.

For another thing, this revelation tells us of eternal life which is quality rather than quantity. John says that it begins any time we come to know Jesus. It is not so much a never-ending existence as it is wonder and glory now.

A schoolboy wrote on the examination paper, "The Christian religion allows a man to have only one wife. This is called monotony." There is a better word about marriage from Andre Maurois, who said, "Marriage is a long conversation that always seems too short!" And this is a Johannine revelation of eternity. It is a long conversation, indeed, but it always seems too short to those who have been touched by Christ. And this quality of life, instead of being monotonous, is full of promise and awe.

Then, this revelation shows us that the divine dwells in the human. We try to understand what men are and what humanity means. We talk about the divinity of Jesus Christ, but we are only using words to describe something that words cannot describe. Was Jesus the perfect man? And is man divine when he is as he ought to be? G. K. Chesterton helped me in this. When he was a young man he wrote:

> There was a man who dwelt in the east centuries ago,
> And now I cannot look at a sheep or a sparrow,
> A lily or a cornfield, a raven or a sunset,
> A vineyard or a mountain without thinking of him;
> If this be not to be divine, what is it?

Finally, John tells us of the ultimate victory which God brings to life. Violence and evil make life cheap. So John brings us the great word, "In the world you will have trouble. But courage! The victory is mine; I have conquered the world" (John 16:33). In his book, *Caesar and Christ,* Will Durant said, "There is no greater drama in human record than the sight of a few Christians, scorned and oppressed by a succession of emperors, bearing all trials with a fierce tenacity, multiplying quietly, building order while their enemies generated chaos, fighting the sword with the word, brutality with hope, and at last defeating the strongest state that history has known. Caesar and Christ met in the arena, and Christ had won." That is the good news of John.

WHO WAS HE?

When all things began, the Word already was.   1:1

The first three gospels are called the "synoptics," because they "see together." They use the same material and their story has the same boundaries. They were written to tell the story of the life of the Messiah. The Gospel of John, however, uses a different vocabulary. It begins with a philosophical discussion which was familiar to the educated people of that period, especially the Greeks. "The Word" means the thought, or the rationality, or the wisdom. John brings together this mighty idea and the person of Jesus, whose life he is going to describe with this underlying assumption—"the Word."

The great word is in the fourteenth verse of the first chapter, where it is written, "So the Word became flesh...." This is the most dramatic and startling expression of the central doctrine of our faith. It is the Christian judgment on all humanistic approaches and philosophies. God is in this story, and God is saying something to the human race about Himself, about us, and about the meaning of life.

In 1961, in *Time* magazine, there was an article about communism in Poland. It told of Professor Schaff, an outstanding Marxist philosopher at the University of Warsaw. Toward the end of one of his classes, Professor Schaff said, a student raised his hand and asked hesitantly, "Professor, I hope you will not be angry with me but could you tell us what you think is the meaning of life?" The professor thought at first that the boy was baiting him, but when he saw the intensity of the expressions on the faces of the rest of the class, he knew he had to answer as best he could. So he talked off the top of his head as the class came to a close. He said he realized at last that this was a question which communism could not evade. What is the meaning of life? It is an inevitable question, and it rises in the minds of communists as well as capitalists. John says at the beginning of his story that Jesus is the clue to the mystery.

WHERE DO YOU LIVE?

> So they went and saw where he was staying, and spent the rest of the day with him. It way then about four in the afternoon.   1:39

Two disciples of John the Baptist, knowing how much he admired Jesus, were curious about where this teacher lived. If they knew where he dwelt, they would have more knowledge about the kind of man he was. Jesus invited them to his place, and they came and visited with him the rest of the day.

It is always important to know where a man lives. The house in the poor section which is at the same time neat and clean says a great deal about the man inside. The rich man's house says something about the rich man's character. Where do we live?

There was an old lady who lived in a basement in the slums. Then she moved into an attic room, where there was light. A neighbor asked her why. She replied, "Oh, you cannot listen to my pastor very long and live in a basement." Neither could you know Jesus Christ and live in the gloom. John Wesley said to poor people in the eighteenth century: "Cleanliness is next to Godliness." His early converts resolved to be clean. The very act of cleaning up their homes spoke of a spiritual transformation that was taking place inside them. You can tell a good deal about a man's spiritual state by finding out where he lives.

Charles Dicken's opening sentence in *Tale of Two Cities* is a classic. "It was the best of times, it was the worst of times, it was the age of wisdom, it was the age of foolishness, it was the epoch of belief, it was the epoch of incredulity, it was the season of Light, it was the season of Darkness, it was the spring of hope, it was the winter of despair, we had everything before us, we had nothing before us, we were all going direct to Heaven, we were all going direct the other way—in short, the period was so far like the present period, that some of its noisiest authorities insisted on its being received for good or for evil, in the superlative degree of comparison only."

Which is a rather long sentence telling us that our point of view is determined by where we live.

WORTHY OF THE NAME

> When Jesus saw Nathanael coming, he said, "Here is an Israelite worthy of the name; there is nothing false in him."   1:47

I was to entertain the annual conference in Lincoln, Nebraska. I wanted to have Professor Halford Luccock as the conference preacher. I wrote to him, and soon I had a letter from him, banged out laboriously on his own typewriter by his own hand. Hal's typing was so bad that I told him I had several friends whose handwriting I could not read but he was the only friend I had whose typing I could hardly read. But his letter was such a joy to receive that I did not realize until the end of it that he had said no to my invitation. But he added, "You are the pastor of St. Paul Methodist Church. Have you ever preached on what a church must be if it is worthy of the name St. Paul?" I had never thought of it, but the ninetieth anniversary of the church was coming very soon and I had my sermon. What must we be to be worthy of the name Christian?

HE KNOWS US!

> He knew men so well, all of them, that he needed no
> evidence from others about a man, for he himself
> could tell what was in a man. 2:24-25

The modern world has faith in computer information. In some
areas this method works, no doubt, but in many situations it is
inadequate. When we are dealing with human beings, we need
to know something of the nature of man, not of computers.
Men are not computers, and we suffer much when we assume
their natures are the same.

John says that Jesus knew human nature and spoke words of
eternal guidance. We are freed from the false idea that Jesus
talked in terms of idealism or assumed that men behave as
angels. The teachings of our Lord reveal the ultimate realist. He
was not just a poet who said sweet things about the human
situation. He was not an idealist talking about how things ought
to be. He is the one who "knew men so well, all of them, that
he needed no evidence from others about a man...." The
preacher is always on the right track when he understands that
whatever Jesus says about human nature is the most realistic
word he will hear.

STARTING OVER

> "In truth, in very truth I tell you, unless a man has
> been born over again he cannot see the kingdom of
> God." 3:3

An artist, showing his picture of a sunset to a critical brother,
was told, "I never saw a sunset like that." The artist smiled and
replied quietly, "No? Don't you wish you could?"

The gospel is as radical as being born anew. It is not a mere reforming at this point or of amending our thoughts. It is a new vision that creates a new man.

We take a new look at ourselves. When Queen Mary tried to put John Knox down by asking, "What are ye within this commonwealth?" he gave a famous reply: "A subject born within the same, Madam. And albeit I neither be earl, lord nor baron within it, yet has God made me (how abject that ever I be in your eyes) a profitable member with the same; yea, Madam, to me it appertains no less to forewarn of such things as may hurt it, if I foresee them, than it does to any of the nobility; for both my vocation and conscience crave plainness of me." A modern historian commented: "Modern democracy was born in that answer."

LOVING THE WORLD

> "God loved the world so much that he gave his only Son...." 3:16

A judgment on all Christian groups who hate the world! There are Christians who believe that they should ignore the physical things of life and deny all of its pleasures. It is a great thing for a man to have in his mind at all time the words: "God loved the world so much."

This gospel, which certainly has elements of Greek influence in it, shows that essentially it is true to its great Hebrew heritage. For this is a Jewish point of view. Some people are shocked at the happy, natural view the Jew takes of the world and of life. The Jew is right. God does not want us to turn our backs on His good gifts. T. H. Huxley, in *A Liberal Education,* was closer to the Fourth Gospel than he knew when he wrote: "For every man the world is as fresh as it was at the first day, and as full of untold novelties for him who has the eyes to see them."

AN HONEST MAN

> "The honest man comes to the light so that it may be
> clearly seen that God is in all he does." 3:21

John Lahr, in *Notes on a Cowardly Lion,* gives us a sketch of his father's life. There was a time when young Bert Lahr fell into the habit of stealing. Finally he was caught taking objects from a hardware store. It was the first his father Jacob or his mother Augusta knew of his thievery. Bert Lahr said of the experience, "I never stole a thing after I got caught at the hardware store. I made up my mind—voom, just like that, when I saw Mom crying in her apron. It was over. Finished." Habits of dishonesty are cured by the light of Christ.

WHO WAS THAT MAN?

> They asked him, "Who is the man who told you to
> take up your bed and walk?" But the cripple who
> had been cured did not know; for the place was
> crowded and Jesus had slipped away. 5:12-13

Who Christ is and what He does for us is easily lost in the crowd. Too many people are around for us to be aware of His presence.

This happens in our relationship with Christ more times than not. A poem by G. A. Studdert-Kennedy tells of crowds who passed Jesus by and ignored him as he walked the streets of Birmingham. He cried for Calvary, preferring crucifixion to neglect. Men still crucify Him, but our common sin is not noticing Him in the crowd and letting Him slip away without realizing he is gone. We do it through the invason of other interests and other activities. We do not have time to worship.

When Habakkuk wrote,

> But the Lord is in his holy temple;
> Let all the earth be hushed in his presence.   (2:20)

he was thinking more of our tendency to forget the presence of
God in the midst of the noise of the world than of a slogan to
put on our bulletins for the worship service. The whole earth is
a temple and God is always in it.

MISSING THE POINT

> "You study the scriptures diligently, supposing that
> in having them you have eternal life; yet, although
> their testimony points to me, you refuse to come to
> me for that life."   5:39-40

Christians often treat the Bible as an end in itself. Just because
we have a Bible, and dust it once a week, we think that we have
obtained righteousness and the good life. Jesus said that the
scriptures point to a life and a Living Presence which can be-
stow the gift of life upon men.

A spoiled little boy managed to evade the servants and made
his way into Winston Churchill's study. "Are you the greatest
man in the world?" he asked. "I certainly am," snapped Sir
Winston. "Now buzz off." This scene in the Fouth Gospel is a
different style and spirit, but the conclusion is the same. Jesus
said that the scriptures point to him as the one who can give
eternal life.

Dean Inge, in his *Studies of English Mystics,* wrote: "In all
questions about religion there is the most distressing divergency.
But the saints do not contradict one another. They claim to have
had glimpses of a land that is very far off, and they prove that
they have been there by bringing back perfectly consistent and
harmonious reports of it." Jesus said, ". . . . their testimony points
to me."

WHO ELSE?

> So Jesus asked the Twelve, "Do you also want to
> leave me?" Simon Peter answered him, "Lord, to
> whom shall we go? Your words are words of eternal
> life."   6:67-68

It was a time of a general falling away and disappointment and
defeat. In great sadness Jesus asked the disciples if they also
wanted to leave him. Then came Peter's great answer, "Lord,
to whom shall we go?" There is here the assumption that they
have to go to someone.

Mr. Malcolm Muggeridge, former editor of *Punch,* has come
to his position as a committed Christian after much wandering
and many questions. He writes, "So I come back to where I
began, to that other King, one *Jesus;* to the Christian notion
that man's efforts to make himself personally and collectively
happy in earthly terms are doomed to failure. He must indeed,
as Christ said, be born again, be a new man, or he is nothing.
So at least I have concluded, after having failed to find in past
experience, present dilemmas and future expectations, any
alternative proposition. As far as I am concerned, it is Christ or
nothing." St. Peter found the same answer.

Dietrich Bonhoeffer had many arguments with his older
brother, Karl Friederich. His brother was an accomplished
skeptic, and he held up before Dietrich the world which science
was revealing and the foolishness of so much, as he regarded it,
fruitless, metaphysical speculation. To his arguments Dietrich
Bonhoeffer replied, in a free translation, "You may knock my
head off, but I shall still believe in God." St. Peter saw that this
ultimate conviction was the only answer to his problems. It
became clear to him when he had to consider an alternate to
Jesus Christ.

SHOCKING

> Jesus was aware that his disciples were murmuring
> about it and asked them, "Does this shock you?"
>
> 6:61

Vital movements make demands on those who join them. Communism's rules of membership sound much like the demands of
the early Christian church, which to the world sounded like a
suicide pact.

Consider some of the demands which minority groups are
putting upon us. They have one thing in common with this
word of Jesus: they are shocking.

When Garibaldi was making his appeal to young Italians to
join with him, he offered them nothing more than a chance to
make sacrifices and probably to die. Churchill, facing the crisis
in 1940, made no promises to the British people: he said he
had nothing to offer but blood, toil, tears and sweat. The demands of a movement that shock people are a sign of its life and
vitality, for only shocking demands move us. J. B. S. Haldane
summed up his experience with Christianity in these words: "I
developed a mild liking for the Anglican ritual and a complete
immunity to religion." If only he had met Jesus Christ and
been shocked!

EDUCATION WITHOUT COLLEGE

> The Jews were astonished: "How is it," they said,
> "that this untrained man has such learning?"   7:15

The Jews of the first century were very like Americans in the
twentieth century. We believe that if a man is to speak with
any authority, he must have a degree from the right college.
We overdo it. Even a college cannot chose its president just on
this basis. It needs a man with experience not only in dealing
with academic matters, but in dealing with people.

The past is a university which every man by necessity has attended. If he has learned to profit from experience and to see what will work and what won't work, he has had as valuable an education as a man who attended schools. Living is an educational process, and the man who has learned from experience need not be ashamed of it, nor should he be overly impressed with academic achievement.

Noel Coward writes in his autobiography that while his body has traveled a good many miles he has the feeling that his mind has not traveled far enough. This is a characteristic that schools and degrees sometimes have, and in this they have very little to contribute.

Jesus was at home in the scriptures, and this in itself was an education. William Lyon Phelps said, "I thoroughly believe in a university education for both men and women; but I believe a knowledge of the Bible without a college course is more valuable than a college course without the Bible." That is a word we have missed.

POLARIZING

Thus he caused a split among the people.   7:43

We talk about influences which are "polarizing." "Polarizing" is a rather high-sounding word that when analyzed means no more than making people choose sides on issues. Every time we come up against a real issue, we polarize. The only kind of issue that does not polarize people is the kind that does not matter one way or another. John says that Jesus "caused a split among the people." One of the accusations hurled against him at the trial was that "his teaching is causing disaffection among the people all through Judaea. It started from Galilee and has spread as far as this city" (Luke 23:5). The King James version reads: "He stirreth up the people."

We had better stop worrying about polarization and be grateful for those issues which make it necessary for people to choose and decide. The church whose only credential is that it brings peace to everybody is not in the Christian tradition. Emerson wrote in his *Journal:* "The Unitarians, born Unitarians, have a pale, shallow religion; but the Calvinist born and reared under his vigorous, aesthetic, scowling creed, when ripened into a Unitarian, becomes powerful, as Dr. Channing, Dewey, Mann, Watson, Garrison and others."

We prefer a situation where we do not have to declare ourselves. But the Old Testament word was, "I offer you the choice of life or death, blessing or curse. Choose life and then you and your descendants will live...'" (Deuteronomy 30:19.) Our religion drives men into a corner. They have to make up their minds and commit themselves. Christianity polarizes.

THE RABBLE

> "As for this rabble, which cares nothing for the Law, a curse is on them." 7:49

Thus speak the aristocratic and the proud. Back of the great revolutions which changed history were the nobility who regarded the common people as rabble. But the French peasants and the Russian peasants, when aroused, overthrew the old systems and started something new.

The despisers of democracy find much to criticize. Yet elections in the midst of troubled times create new faith. "The rabble" have not been as impressed by candidates' attempts to manipulate them as we feared. The general result lifts up our hearts and gives us new faith and courage.

Winston Churchill, in his second volume of *The Second World War,* commented on the magnificent work of the bomb disposal squads during the London blitz. "One squad...consisted of three people—the Earl of Suffolk, his lady private secretary and his rather aged chauffeur. They called themselves 'the holy trinity.' Their prowess and continued existence got around among all who knew. Thirty-four unexploded bombs did they tackle with urbane and smiling efficiency. But the thirty-fifth claimed its forfeit. Up went the Earl of Suffolk and his holy trinity. But we may be sure that, as for Greatheart, all the trumpets sounded for them on the other side." Indeed, in crisis, "the rabble," with the aristocrats who joined them, came' through, as they have for two thousand years. Most of the early Christians and the Saints were "the rabble."

NO PROPHETS FROM GALILEE

> ". . . you will find that prophets do not come from Galilee."   7:52

They had made up their minds, and when Nicodemus challenged them, and said that their law, which they were so anxious to quote, did not permit them to pass judgment on a man until he had had a hearing, this was their reply. We have made up our minds, they seemed to be saying, do not confuse us with facts. They knew that prophets never came out of Galilee.

We take care of a good many situations without a hearing of any kind because we have made up our minds about them beforehand. Remember the brilliant inventor who was asked the secret of his discoveries. He replied, "I challenged maxims."

Our closed-mind attitude operates toward people who come from the wrong side of the tracks, and from homes that have less luxury than our own. We have no time to listen to such people or respect them. We do it in churches, and in some WASP communities. Catholics suffer because we have decided without thought that no good thing can come from them. There are sects who minister primarily to the poor and the uneducated. We dismiss anyone who comes from those groups.

One of the joys of my ministry has been the discovery of heroes in unexpected places. One of God's wonderful surprises is to bring us face to face with a prophet from Galilee.

NO WANDERING IN THE DARK

> "No follower of mine shall wander in the dark; he
> shall have the light of life."   8:12

I remember meeting with a group of Christians who spent the evening testifying to guidance that the Lord had given them in specific situations. One salesman claimed that he always knew when to call upon a prospect because the Lord told him. Another man said that he was saved unnecessary journeys because he was told ahead of time whether the journey was necessary and would be fruitful. I listened in despair because nothing like that had ever happened to me.

The young David Hume became the secretary of a General in his young manhood because he was persuaded that this experience would be good for him before settling down to his studies. But he found nothing but inefficiency and corruption in the way the British handled the war with the French over Canada. Of the War Secretary and his hopeless bungling the common saying was, "He lost half an hour every morning and spent the day searching for it." That could be said of some preachers, and it is often the main characteristic of consciously busy people.

Jesus says that our lives need not be a wandering around in the confusion of darkness. He gives us his light and we see what the main purpose of living ought to be. We will still run into many mysteries and fears and despairs, but following him sets us on the right track. He gives us a sense of direction and makes clear the immediate task. We have no right to ask for more.

HOME AT LAST!

"Your home is in this world, mine is not." 8:23

The man who takes this world too seriously is always trying to be up to date. He wants the latest style, the latest book, and the latest music. Instead of finding dignity and significance, he flutters from one fad to another like a butterfly. Where is our home? The hymn has the answer:

> O God, our help in ages past,
> Our hope for years to come,
> Our shelter from the stormy blast,
> And our eternal home!

SINNERS ARE SLAVES

"In very truth I tell you," said Jesus, "that everyone who commits sin is a slave." 8:34

"To sin" in Greek means "to miss the mark." But this word of Jesus is the Christian interpretation, although it is a rather startling one to us. Sin is slavery.

The popular interpretation is that sin is rebellion and excitement. It appeals to the young and the adventurous because being sinful is going against the establishment. It appears preferable over tiresome virtue. The devil in "Paradise Lost" is more exciting than the saints.

But Jesus says that sin is slavery. We are not our own masters and we cannot fulfill our own desires. We become the sad creature St. Paul describes in the seventh chapter of Romans: we do what we do not want to do and are not being able to do what we really want to do.

The sinner is the man in the grip of evil impulses he cannot control. He follows a dark way with no knowledge of what waits around the next corner. He finds his behavior driving him to death and destruction.

William Cullen Bryant wrote some lines about the way a man ought to die:

> So live that . . .
> Thou go not, like the quarry-slave at night,
> Scourged to his dungeon . . .

He was talking about death, but his lines describe the sinner and his way of life.

PEOPLE, NOT SPECTACLES

"Is not this the man who used to sit and beg?"　9:9

The people had seen this man begging at the temple for years, but no one apparently had ever shown any interest in him, or taken the time to know him as a man. He was a spectacle.

As Arthur Schopenhauer grew older he grew less and less sociable. "Were I a king," he said, "my prime command would be—leave me alone." He spoke for a good many people in those words, for we do not want to be involved and we do not want to be bothered.

How easily we can get used to things! I was in Hong Kong some time ago and a man told me that I ought to see the homeless people who slept at night on the sidewalks of a certain street. He said it was most "interesting." We get used to misery, and with too much familiarity there is bred in us contempt for the suffering.

THIS IS ALL I KNOW

> "All I know is this: once I was blind, now I can see."
>
> 9:25

There is no better illustration of the conflict between the plain man and the scholar or academic theologian than this story of Jesus' healing the blind man. The Pharisees wanted to know if the healer was legitimate and had the right credentials to heal. The man who had been healed cared nothing about these questions. He only knew that he could see, where formerly he was blind. This witness has authority, and his is the kind of testimony which has formed the power of the Christian church.

St. Patrick said there are three orders of saints. First, there are those who are a glory on the mountain tops. Second, there are those who are gleams on the sides of the hills. Third, there are those who are just a few faint lights down in the valleys. The third group of saints are the majority, and their witness comes from people who are blind and who can now see a few faint lights in the ordinary life in the valleys. This man who was healed was one of them.

WHO ARE YOU TO GIVE US LESSONS?

> "If that man had not come from God he could have done nothing." "Who are you to give us lessons," they retorted, "born and bred in sin as you are?" Then they expelled him from the synagogue.
>
> 9:33-34

A man who had been healed and whose eyes had been opened was not persuaded that the one who had performed the miracle was a bad man. He assumed that the kind of thing that had happened to him was from God. But the Pharisees would have none of this common sense from a plain man, and they expelled him from the synagogue.

Confucius, the Chinese sage, who lived sometime around 500 B.C., said: "I live in a very small house, but my windows look out on a very large world." It is not unusual to find a man who lives in a small house with a very wide and profound vision. Neither is it unusual to see a man who lives in a very luxurious house whose point of view is narrow, selfish, and mean. Something that had happened to this man in the story had opened his eyes to the splendor of Jesus and his work. But the trained men from their point of vantage were looking out only through the narrow windows of their own law and their own training.

BE HONEST

> Some Pharisees in his company asked, "Do you mean that we are blind?" "If you were blind," said Jesus, "you would not be guilty, but because you say 'We see,' your guilt remains."   9:40-41

Noel Coward said: "These glib, over-articulate and amoral preachers force their lives into fantastic shapes and problems because they cannot help themselves. Impelled chiefly by the impact of their personalities each upon the other, they are like moths in a pool of light, unable to tolerate the lonely outer darkness, and equally unable to share the light without colliding constantly and bruising one another's wings" (*A Talent to Amuse,* by Sheridan Morley, Doubleday, 1969, p. 225). A good description of people who pretend to know what they do not know and to be what they are not.

I called my doctor and tried to describe a minor ache. I asked him, "Doctor, what causes it?" He said, "I haven't the foggiest idea." Instead of weakening my confidence in him, his answer increased it tenfold. I have complete faith in that man for his honesty and lack of pretense. He gives the plain truth always, as far as his training and skill enables him to see it.

There is what might be called the "promotion type." They live on the basis of an overly optimistic view of the future. Get away from them as fast as you can and never trust a word they say. They cause harm, and their pretenses cause unimaginable tragedies. Christ saves us from this trap.

ADVENTURE STORY

"How long must you keep us in suspense?"   10:24

The gospel is a suspense story. In earlier days when I was a pastor, on Saturday nights I stayed home, went to bed early, and read mysteries. I felt guilty about this until I read Christopher Morley's remark that liking detective stories was the sign of a cultivated mind.

How can we think of the gospel as a detective story? Well, for one thing, who killed Jesus, and who were the guilty murderers? Just this group or that group? That debate has been going on for a long time. Research has proved that the Jewish people were not to blame. The old Negro spiritual, "Were you there when they crucified my Lord?," finds me saying in shame, "Yes, I was there, and I have done many things in my lifetime to associate myself with that crime."

How is it going to turn out in the end? The story is clear enough when it comes to the resurrection. But has the resurrection found me? On which side of the resurrection do I actually live? Will I be able to discover it and live as one who has been saved from death? How will the gospel affect our world, and what will Christ do in the future?

SATISFACTION GUARANTEED
OR YOUR MONEY BACK

> "If I am not acting as my Father would, do not believe
> me."   10:37

Sales propositons on television and in the newspapers guarantee
that if the product is not as the advertisement promised, we can
get our money back. Jesus said that if he did not act as they
would expect God to act, then they were free to disbelieve him.

What man in all history ever dared to lay his authority on
the line as he did? Any man who would dare do such a thing
would make himself the laughing-stock of his own period and
condemn himself to oblivion after he died. But this word still
stands as one we read and believe. Through the years there has
grown a faith in the "Christlike God."

Dick Van Dyke says that if he were looking for a Sunday
School teacher he would run the following ad, "Wanted:
Teacher. Must have the wisdom of Solomon, the patience of
Job, and the courage of David. Must teach like St. Paul, lead
like Moses, and stay cool under fire like Shadrach." We never
find such a teacher, but Jesus dared to put his whole claim of
authority upon the basis of his daily behavior. Finding God in
the man who walked and never grew faint, who confronted his
mortal enemies, and who faced death with courage is such an
awe-inspiring experience that all we can do is bow our heads
and say, "God was in Christ."

THEOLOGY BECAME BIOGRAPHY

> "I know that he will rise again," said Martha, "at the
> resurrection on the last day." Jesus said, "I am the
> resurrection. . . ." 11:24-25

Great events of faith which were to take place in the other
world are brought into this present time through Jesus. Martha
represented Judaism when she said she believed in resurrection
on the last day. But it is a radical new word when Jesus says,
"I am the resurrection."

Tenzing Norkay, the Sherpa herdsman and expedition guide
in the 1953 Everest expedition, said about reaching the top of
Everest, "I thought of God and the greatness of His work. I
have a feeling for climbing to the top and there making worship
closer to God. Not the same feeling of English Sahib who wants
only to conquer the mountain. I feel more like making pil-
grimage." And it was this feeling that came to the people who
were in the presence of Jesus and saw him through the eyes of
St. John. It was a feeling of worship, and the assurance that
God had drawn close to them.

When Eugène Ionesco was elected to the Académie Française,
a newspaper reporter interviewing him asked if he were surprised when he was given this highest honor. Ionesco replied
quickly, "Yes, I was surprised. But, you know," he added after
a little reflection, "I am always surprised. I go through life
perpetually astonished at everything that happens around me."
This happened to people who walked with the Lord, and to
Martha there came this revelation that the One whom her
brother and sister loved so much was himself the doctrine of
the resurrection fulfilled. It is in Jesus himself that theology
and Christian doctrine became biography.

STOP WORRYING

> "Then the Romans will come and sweep away our
> temple. . . ."   11:48

Somebody is always worrying that the church will be destroyed
by an action of some person. To them the main thing is to keep
the system alive and eliminate anything that threatens its destruction.

We live in a dangerous world, and many are the prophecies
that foretell the limited length of time the church has left. They
remind me of that strange story in the Old Testament, about
the man who put out his hand to steady the Ark. The lesson
seems to be that the Ark does not need our hand to steady it
and the church we join is not dependent upon us for life. We
need the faith to know that neither the Romans nor anyone
else can sweep away a temple where God dwells.

We get our values reversed. The institution exists to pass
along to the next generation the experience. If we save the institution we save just a symbol of the reality. We must be concerned about the inner spiritual reality itself. If we maintain
the truth of Jesus Christ, the church will take care of itself.

A five-year-old Sunday School girl, when asked what she
learned from the miracle of Jesus turning water into wine at
the wedding feast, said: "When you have a wedding, it's a good
idea to have Jesus there too!" The main thing to know about
the religious institution is that Jesus is there. Stop worrying.

SPEAKING FOR THE ESTABLISHMENT

> He did not say this of his own accord, but as the High
> Priest in office that year. . . .   11:51

As soon as a man becomes a part of the establishment, he needs
to be on his guard lest he set his allegiance to that group first
and his loyalty to Christ second. Every man who is an official in

the life of the church goes through this temptation and faces this difficulty. I speak with some experience of the subject, and I wonder how many times I would have said what I did if I had not been a bishop of the church.

This is the conflict between the priest and the prophet which is so sharp in the Old Testament. Let us have some sympathy for the priest. He is the man who is responsible for an institution, and he is the man who works with the people day by day. He is not always free to say what he would like to say, because he has to consider his responsibility to the church. The prophet had no institution for which he was responsible, and he preached wherever he felt called to proclaim his truth. Oftentimes he was in the marketplace, but he would move on from there to a new situation. The problem is to be a priest and yet not lose the prophetic insight.

Speaking of Ralph Waldo Emerson, Oliver Wendell Holmes remarked that "Here was an iconoclast without a hammer, who took down his idols from their pedestal so tenderly that it seemed like an act of worship." Not a bad description of a man with a deep sense of responsibility. For Emerson also had a respect for plain speech and sincerity. After he delivered a lecture at Middlebury College, the presiding minister offered this concluding prayer: "We beseech Thee, O Lord, to deliver us from ever hearing any more such transcendental nonsense as we have just listened to from this sacred desk." Asked to comment on this public insult, Emerson's only remark was, "The minister seems a very conscientious, plain-spoken gentleman." It is not easy to belong to the establishment and at the same time remember that one is an ordinary man subject to honest criticism like anybody else.

A MEAN VIRTUE

> At this, Judas Iscariot, a disciple of his—the one who
> was to betray him—said, "Why was this perfume
> not sold for thirty pounds and given to the poor?"
> He said this, not out of any care for the poor, but
> because he was a thief. . . .   12:4-6

Every time the church spends money on beautifying its sanc-
tuary, someone will refuse to pledge to the project, saying that
the money ought to go to the poor. Judas raised this same cry
against Mary when she anointed the feet of Jesus with her
costly ointment. People who make the loudest cry about matters
of this kind do not give to any cause whatsoever if it is possible.
And so John analyzes this word of Judas by simply saying he
did not object "out of any care for the poor, but because he was
a thief."

It is discouraging to note the number of church members
who limit their giving to the smallest amount possible for them
to still be regarded as respectable members. A four-year-old
watched carefully as the parishioners dropped their cash in the
plate and then said to his father, "Don't pay for me, dad. Remember I'm under five."

Some are not actually thieves; they simply have no ability to
appreciate the generous act and the impulsive courtesy. They
cannot comprehend the love of Mary and her desire to give to
Christ. Herbert Spencer, the philosopher, visited Niagara Falls,
the honeymooners' paradise. He wrote this about its grandeur:
"The fall is a hundred and sixty feet high; it is calculated that it
delivers one hundred million tons of water per hour, or more
than twenty-seven thousand per second. . . . This mass of water,
as it curls over, is probably some twenty feet thick. . . . At the
bottom it is subject to a lateral pressure of, say, fifteen pounds
to the square inch. . . . Hence the rocks on which it falls have
to bear the brunt of, say twenty thousand tons per second, mov-
ing with a velocity of more than one hundred feet per second."

What is there to say about a man who sets down such prosaic words in the midst of beauty? Judas had a streak of this in him, and it was a part of his sickness.

Always sensitive to the spontaneous act of generosity, Jesus would not have it criticized. This part of life is most important, and if we allow it to be pushed out of our minds by more "practical" impulses we have become very poor indeed. It is discouraging to find a man who is a thief or who is unable to comprehend the lovely act or gesture sounding like a practical man giving good reasons for his meanness and smallness.

HOW CAN THEY FIGHT AN IDEA?

> The chief priests then resolved to do away with Lazarus as well, since on his account many Jews were going over to Jesus and putting their faith in him.   12:10-11

The Pharisees, in their blind hatred of Jesus, resolved to destroy Lazarus, whose only fault was that he had been raised by Jesus. In Germany the wrath of the Nazi party turned against Christian people who had no desire to fight against the government. So that little fellowship in Finkenwalde of which Dietrich Bonhoeffer was a member was put into danger, and they never knew what their fate would be from hour to hour. Bonhoeffer said simply, "We accept every day as a gift from God."

The Pharisees are like the secret police of a tyranny, trying to ferret out anyone whose life and faith could be a threat to the established order. And as the Pharisees put it to one another, "You see you are doing no good at all; why, all the world has gone after him!" (John 12:19).

In the constant struggle between true religion and the state, the state is blind; it still has confidence in the weapons it used in other times and other places. But as Victor Hugo said, nothing is so powerful as an idea whose time has come. The conflict always ends in victory for the unarmed Christ and his witnesses.

HOW TO FIND YOURSELF

> "The man who loves himself is lost. . . ."   12:25

Self-respect is a precious possession, and we must not interpret this verse falsely. The old Scotch weaver prayed, "Help me O Lord to have a good opinion of myself." The common possession of men who have contributed to society has been a high sense of self-respect.

But woe unto the man who does not go beyond this in his outreach. Nothing is more miserable than the man whose whole attention is on himself and his own mood. To become one of those tiresome persons whose whole world is limited by their own ego is a fate we should not wish on anyone.

At the end of the day it is the good we have done and the character we have achieved that measure us. When a man regards himself as the final value, he is not likely to accomplish much good and he will achieve no character. In a strange kind of paradox, we are to love every human being, but "the man who loves himself is lost." This is serendipity. What we really want comes to us when we do not make it our goal.

REPUTATION, OR GOD'S WILL?

> For they valued their reputation with men rather than the honour which comes from God.   12:43

A French premier made a cynical remark about politics. "The art of politics," he said, "lies not in finding solutions to fundamental problems, but in keeping quiet those who raise them."

This saves our reputation with men, but it cuts us off from the honor of God.

The acceptance of the prevailing mood as a standard has caused much disaster. There are not many people that are aware of God's command who are willing to be guided by it. In *Cities on the Move* (Oxford University Press, 1970), Arnold Toynbee says, "Man allows himself to be victimized by the artificial environment that he has created for himself by his technological prowess. The... tragedy is that he could save himself from at least the direst of the consequences of this self-victimization if he were to allow his foresight to get the better of his inertia, instead of waiting, as he does wait, frequently til the eleventh hour and sometimes til the thirteenth, before rousing himself to cope with the evils of his own making. . . ."

Most great men have taken the opinions of their contemporaries rather lightly but held with great tenacity to their own principles.

JESUS THE JUDGE

> "There is a judge for the man who rejects me and does not accept my words; the word that I spoke will be his judge on the last day."   12:48

The little boy who was trying to explain the difference between God the Creator and Jesus the Savior put it in this brief word, "God puts you down and Jesus takes you up."

But in this verse there is a warning that even the words of Jesus will be our judge at the last day. Gentleness and forgiveness are real elements in our experience of Christ, but there is a severity in him that we must not miss for our own salvation.

Roger Williams, the great champion of religious liberty in the New World, was a vigorous, controversial man, and an irritating nuisance. He told about a ship that had on board a very obnoxious passenger who claimed to know that ahead there was a hidden reef. He told the captain, who would not listen to a mere layman. The man continued to tell the other passengers, but they were annoyed by his constant warning. Finally they threw him overboard and, as Williams put it, "This energetic measure put an end to all remonstrances, and nothing could be more touching than a unanimity that reigned on board." But suddenly the vessel ran aground on the reef and sank. Williams added, "They had drowned the giver of the warning but the reef remained." Christians are sometimes like the Greeks who killed the messengers who brought bad news. Let us look again at these words of our Lord, "The word that I spoke will be his judge on the last day."

TRAITOR IN THE FAMILY

> After saying this, Jesus exclaimed in deep agitation of spirit, "In truth, in very truth I tell you, one of you is going to betray me." 13:21

Leaving for the moment all discussion of what prompted Judas to betray Christ, let us think of the other side of that picture. Jesus had to experience the betrayal of one of his disciples, one of his friends. It is his association with all of us who have had or will know this experience we must understand.

Sometimes the betrayal of a principle which we have held with endurance comes from someone as close to us as the disciple was to Jesus. Queen Victoria became concerned with the reckless spending of one of her grandsons. She was upset especially when he wrote to her reminding her of his approaching birthday and suggesting that some money would be a most acceptable gift. In her own hand she answered, sternly reproving him for his extravagance and urging upon him the practice of economy. His reply staggered her. "Dear Grandma," he said, "Thank you for your kind letter of advice. I have sold the same for five pounds." It is not reported what she said or what she did.

Sir Walter Scott learned that, due to the failure of a publishing company, he was responsible for a debt of one hundred and thirty thousand pounds. Refusing help from anybody, he simply shouldered the obligation and began to write under such terrific pressure that he hastened his death. He refused to escape the debt by taking the bankruptcy road. Scott has been an inspiration to people for over a hundred years, and he has given us an example of a man who accepted a terrific debt laid upon him through no fault of his own. Toward the end of his life, Scott wrote to a friend, "We are pilgrims for a season; the evening is necessarily the weariest and the most over-clouded portion of our march; but while the purpose is firm and the will good, the journey may be endured, and in God's good time we shall reach its end, footsore and heartsore perhaps but neither disheartened nor dishonored." (Pearson, *Sir Walter Scott,* Harper, 1954). This great man's inspiration must have come through his contemplation of the hurt and the courage of his Lord who suffered betrayal.

CURE FOR TROUBLED HEARTS

"Set your troubled hearts at rest."   14:1

A stanza from an old hymn keeps ringing in my mind:

> Now rest, my long divided heart;
> Fixed on this blissful center, rest:
> Here have I found a nobler part;
> Here heavenly pleasures fill my breast.

Philip Doddridge wrote this hymn in the eighteenth century. It seems to be an echo of this verse in St. John.

How great is this promise of a troubled heart at rest! A "Millerite" came to Emerson, very much upset and alarmed. "Do you know that tonight the world is coming to an end?"

was his agitated greeting. All Emerson did was smile and reply, "I am very glad to hear it. Man will get along better without it." The Christians who spend their lives running around agitated and upset are a denial of their profession.

John Wesley, on his way to Georgia as a young, troubled pastor, was profoundly influenced by a group of German missionaries on their way to the New World. With faith and calm courage they faced danger in the midst of a terrible storm which threatened the destruction of the ship. They seemed to be at ease and untroubled.

Hudson, the missionary to China, was brought the disturbing news that one of his mission stations had been destroyed and some of his co-workers killed. A short time later he went about his work, humming a hymn. One of his co-workers objected to his singing, saying that it showed poor taste and callousness of spirit. Hudson's reply was, "Would it help them if I worried and despaired?" When Ignatius Loyola was asked what he would do if the Pope proscribed his order and ended his activity, he replied that he would pray for fifteen minutes and then he would go on as if nothing had happened. One of the greatest gifts that Jesus gives us is the power to set the troubled hearts at rest.

FRIEND AT COURT

> ". . . and he will give you another to be your Advocate. . . ." 14:16

Jesus took the word "Advocate" from the Jewish law court, to help his disciples understand what he was saying. The advocate was a person of good standing who had the confidence of the court. He would present the case in the best possible light, and he would give personal support to the prisoner. This, says Jesus, is what the Holy Spirit does.

Life is a trial. Each day finds us having to give testimony for our mistakes and failings. It is a trial for our life, in which we feel that probably we shall be found guilty. Having someone who will take our part and strengthen us in our adversity is more than we deserve. But this is the mercy and hope which Jesus offers to those who follow him.

The teacher in an integrated Sunday School in Washington asked her children, "What do you think when you see the church doors open to everyone who wants to worship God here?" A little black girl gave an unforgettable answer. "It's like walking into the heart of God," she said. This is the experience of the man under condemnation who has to face it alone. Suddenly, the Advocate is there with him. The Advocate will not soften the facts of the case, but his presence and support means everything to the man on trial.

A Methodist minister who had been guilty of "unministerial conduct," and had made a fool of himself, was sentenced to face a committee of his peers and receive their judgment. That judgment was that he must stand before the members of the annual conference while the bishop pronounced the judgment of the church on such behavior. The time came, and the man stood by himself before his brethren and waited for the bishop to reveal to them all his foolishness and his guilt. Then one of the leading members of the conference simply went forward, put his hand on the man's shoulder, and shared the condemnation. The conference that day came to understand what having an advocate meant for every sinner.

WHEN YOU ARE READY

> "There is still much that I could say to you, but the
> burden would be too great for you now."   16:12

Man plays an important part in the process of revelation,
although it is difficult to keep clear. Theology moves like a
sailing ship, tacking with the wind, and it is sometimes too far
to the right or to the left. John Calvin was so committed to the
idea of the sovereignty of God that he probably overdid man's
helplessness and inability to act. Karl Barth was restoring the
balance to humanistic theology when he implied that man can
do nothing but wait until God acts. A profounder truth comes
from St. Augustine, whose clear word was that without God
we cannot, but without us God will not. God has to wait until
we are able to hear what He says.

I think back to my father and mother, who often said things
which I simply could not understand. Mark Twain said that
when he was fourteen years old his father seemed so ignorant
he could hardly stand to have the old man around. Then he
added that when he was twenty he thought it was remarkable
how much his father seemed to have learned in just six years.
But the change is not in our fathers, it is in ourselves. At long
last what they tried in vain to make us comprehend, suddenly
we see.

TROUBLE OF COURSE, BUT VICTORY!

> "In the world you will have trouble. But courage!
> The victory is mine; I have conquered the world."
>   16:33

This is one of the great passages in the Bible, and it is the
triumphant promise of Jesus to those who follow him. To begin

with he says that we are going to have trouble. There is no attempt to gloss it over or to make us think it will be different. Our Lord never makes the slightest attempt to say that following him is going to be easy. He begins with the affirmation, "In the world you will have trouble."

But lest this begin to weigh us down too much, his second word to us is "Courage." We ought not to be too upset by this warning of trouble. The unhappiest people in the world are those who have made themselves secure and find it boring. It is not trouble that defeats men, but monotony. Any man whose life has been full of action knows that life without danger would be robbed of wonder. As Harry Kemp put it, "The poor man is not he who is without a cent, but he who is without a dream." The psychiatrists' patients have too much, while the poor, whose life is demanding and hard, are well.

Then Jesus says that the victory is his; he has attained it for us. The war may not be over, but the decisive battle has been fought and won. "I have conquered the world," is his closing word.

Some years ago, in La Paz, Bolivia, there lived Dr. Frank Beck, a missionary whose life was similar in some ways to Albert Schweitzer's. When Dr. Beck was thirty-five years old he saw that the people he wanted to serve in Bolivia needed a doctor. So he went back to Northwestern Medical School and became a doctor. He gave his life to the Indians of Bolivia and won the respect and love of all the people. He tried to retire three or four times, but each time he was called back to go on a little while longer. Finally, after his last retirement, he said to his wife as they left for the plane, "It's been fun, hasn't it?" I thought of that when I held his funeral, and I thought that this is the sign of victory. Life for Dr. Frank Beck was never easy. It was always full of trouble, and he had to do his work with limited resources. But there was joy in his heart. He is one of the people I have known who achieved victory. Jesus promised it to all of his disciples.

ETERNAL LIFE IS NOW

> "This is eternal life: to know thee who alone art truly God, and Jesus Christ whom thou hast sent." 17:3

Here is one of the most radical ideas you will find anywhere. Eternal life is not a matter of quantity, but of quality. It is not a mattter of length, but of style. The brief life of our Lord illustrates pre-eminently that this verse is a testimony to the true nature of "eternal life."

It begins now and we do not have to wait to claim it. Wherever I am, if I have met Jesus Christ, eternal life begins. The Gospel of John grasps this truth supremely.

This eternal life is the guarantee for all the promises which we find in the gospel. We do not have to wait until death before we may claim it. This ought to be the Easter message which the church gives the world.

John Knox, finding his way through to the Reformation affirmation, said of the seventeenth chapter of John, "This is where I cast my first anchor." It was to him the center of his faith and his proclamation, and it ought to be ours.

STRANGERS IN THE WORLD

> "....they are strangers in the world, as I am." 17:14

A newly arrived preacher asked a small boy the way to the post office. The boy gave him the directions and the minister thanked him, saying, "You come to church next Sunday and I'll show you the way to heaven." The boy shook his head dubiously, "How can you show me the way to heaven," he asked, "when you can't even find the post office?" Christians are strangers to some things here, but wise in those matters that have to do with heaven and the life eternal. We know little about practical things like making money, and so much about things which give life its meaning. Strangers on the earth but quite at home in the spiritual realm: that is not a bad description of saints.

Let us not give the impression that a Christian is so "spiritual" that he has no acquaintance with failure and no knowledge of defeat. When Leslie Weatherhead finished his year as president of the British Methodist Church, some of his reflections and observations were published in the Methodist Recorder magazine. He thought that one of the main reasons for the modern pulpit's weakness was that there was too much preaching about the "Ideal" and not enough about a man's day by day experiences in trying to follow Christ. The layman gets the impression that the Christian experience ought to be a constant succession of glorious victories, instead of the mixed bag we know it to be. Neither preachers nor other Christians are strangers to daily mental and spiritual failures. But we never settle down and assume that we ought to feel at home in the world. To that notion we are strangers, for we belong to two different worlds and orders.

C. P. Snow in 1935 began a sequence of novels under the general theme, *Strangers and Brothers.* The closing volume of the series was published in 1970, with the title *Last Things.* Christians are not strangers in A. E. Houseman's sense:

> I, a stranger and afraid
> In a world I never made.   (Last Poems, XII)

They are, as C. P. Snow phrased it: "Strangers and Brothers" on their way to their Father's house.

I WAS SENT

"...these men know that thou didst send me."   17:25

One of the heroic stories of early Methodism in Germany is of German converts from America returning to their native land to start the Methodist Church. One man, beginning his ministry in a great seaport city and having a difficult time, said that he found it hard to proclaim the Word in that city, where some of Germany's greatest preachers held forth. But, he said, what kept up his courage was that he had not come of himself; he had been sent.

One thing hard to understand is the word of some radical theologians: They say that they know nothing about God, all that is demanded of us that we "follow Jesus." But Jesus was aware from the beginning that he was sent by God. Our Lord never claimed any other authority but that he was doing God's will. The early church was built on this foundation.

It is a great thing, when among strangers, to be representing somebody besides yourself. Ambassadors abroad do not stand on their own authority; they speak for their country. We do not speak for ourselves; we stand on the authority of the gospel. We become like Caspar Milquetoast in the classic picture. The poor, uncertain, woebegone man is standing on the streetcorner in the rain. Finally, he pulls down his old hat, his old, rainsoaked hat, and says, "Well, I'll wait one more hour and if he doesn't come then, he can go borrow the hundred dollars from somebody else."

It was the dignity and strength of Christ's authority that gave the martyrs their might. It is the lack of it that makes the church lose its way and become merely apologetic. The power of the Christian church lies in its faith that, to the extent that it belongs to Jesus Christ, it belongs to God.

YOUR OWN IDEA?

> Jesus said, "Is that your own idea, or have others suggested it to you?"   18:34

There must come a time when the Christian knows from his own experience whereof he speaks. When we are in school we quote authorities, because we have had no experience. The less sure we are of an authentic Christian experience, the more we quote others. But when a man can say, "I know this, for I have found it true for myself," he stands at the beginning of his power as a witness.

Carlyle said, "What this parish needs is a man who knows God at more than second hand." Such a man is always needed by a generation, and by a church. When it can be said of us, as it was said of Jesus, that he spoke not as a scribe but as one who had authority, then comes the time of our true usefulness.

You find witnesses in very humble places, and I have heard the testimony of an uneducated man who carried tremendous force. There has been much debate regarding John Wesley's "heartwarming" experience, but one thing is clear: After he had been through that experience, he spoke with a new authority.

Henry David Thoreau wrote: "To know that we know what we know, and that we do not know what we do not know is true knowledge." When we can speak great truths out of our own experience, we are saved from doubts and given authority.

GIVE US THE BANDIT

> **Again the clamour rose; "Not him; we want Barab-
> bas!" (Barabbas was a bandit.)**   18:40

The people who expressed a preference for a bandit over Jesus Christ seem to us to have been hopelessly blind and unresponsive. Thank goodness, we are likely to say, things have changed since that time. But have they really changed?

The practical worship of ruthless killers is the story of human history. Napoleon brought suffering to many people, but he still has an honored place whenever we think of the past. If a man brings victory to a nation, he can be forgiven anything.

If, in the realm of business life, a tough, ruthless, conscienceless bandit makes millions of dollars at the expense of ruined men and their families, still we prefer him. As Leo Durocher put it, "Nice guys finish last." It is only long after the bandit is gone that the honest biography appears, showing the selfishness and the evil of the popular hero. The truth is that in this field, as in the world of military adventure, Barabbas is often our choice over Jesus Christ.

J. B. S. Haldane was not religious according to his own estimate, but he was deeply sensitive to human values. He had great respect for the virtues of courage and the comradeship of men living and dying for a common cause. But as he grew older, he became more and more a bitter critic of the governmental policies of England and of "a civilization in which people take refuge in war from the worries of everyday life and peace." Barabbas appeals always to those who are looking for some escape from their everyday routine.

But when a man sees the heroism of our Lord and the courage of his life, he finds one who seems more heroic, more courageous, and more worthy of allegiance than Barabbas.

MIND YOUR OWN BUSINESS

> When he caught sight of him, Peter asked, "Lord, what will happen to him?" Jesus said, "If it should be my will that he wait until I come, what is it to you? Follow me."
> 21:21-22

Jesus foretold Peter's future and the manner of his death. Then Peter looked around and, seeing John, asked what was going to happen to him. Abruptly Jesus answered and although I take some liberties with the translation, he said to Peter, in effect, "Mind your own business."

A good word for all those who worry about matters that are not their concern. The gossip spends long hours ferreting out scandal which most people do not want to hear, because most people do not consider it any of their business. Shortly after his election as President of the United States, Calvin Coolidge was asked the secret of his success in politics. "It was very simple," he drawled. "I just listened my way along." Not bad advice for a Christian.

Said Herbert Butterfield, the historian: "Follow Christ and to everything else, be uncommitted." This simplifies a man's life and keeps his eye on the main issues.

I DID NOT TELL THE HALF OF IT

> There is much else that Jesus did. If it were all to be recorded in detail, I suppose the whole world could not hold the books that would be written.   21:25

What a wonderful conclusion! It sounds like the words of Marco Polo, whose tales of his travels were doubted by most of his hearers. When he was dying, his spiritual adviser asked him if before he died he did not want to confess that his stories had been exaggerations and lies, so he would clear the record before appearing before God. Marco Polo's only reply was, "I did not tell the half of it." So John says at the end of his book, "I did not tell but a small part of the truth about Jesus Christ.

Who could write down everything that Jesus did? The great deeds which had their inspiration in Christianity are so numerous that, as John puts it, "The whole world could not hold the books that would be written." Even the people who have been inspired by Christ may not know where the inspiration originated. But because Jesus has not so much influenced our civilization as "been ploughed into it," his presence is everywhere.

When we trace where most of the values in our civilization came from, it amazes us to find that they came from Christ. Education; hospitals; women's lib; children's welfare; libraries; care for the poor, the sick, and the unfortunate come from him.

Who could find room for all the books which might be written about it all?

Every preacher has instances of personal influence beyond his knowledge which happened when he was unaware that any virtue had gone from him. A boy says, "I heard you preach these words and it changed my life." A man says, "I was fighting a hard battle against a temptation and I heard you speak a word that gave me the victory." A woman says, "I had a broken heart and you healed it." A preacher comes to the place where the influence he wields is too heavy a burden to carry. And if this is true of men like us, who are evil and weak, how much more is it true of the influence of Jesus! For us, John's conclusion is also an introduction.

JUSTICE AND MERCY

> Jesus bent down and wrote with his finger on the ground. When they continued to press their question he sat up straight and said, "That one of you who is faultless shall throw the first stone.". . . When they heard what he said, one by one they went away, the eldest first. . . . Jesus again sat up and said to the woman, "Where are they? Has no one condemned you?" She answered, "No one, sir." Jesus said, "Nor do I condemn you. You may go; do not sin again."
>
> 7:6-7, 9, 10-11

Scholars disagree over where this section of the gospel should be placed, but they never argue about its authenticity. It shines in its own light and it belongs truly in a story of Jesus.

A main problem of any society is how to be both merciful and just. Usually the man who insists on justice is lacking in mercy. The lady who had her picture taken objected to it, saying, "I do not think you did me justice." "Madam," was the reply, "you should ask for mercy rather than justice." So should we all.

Our Lord treats people who are strong on justice but weak on mercy by bringing them before themselves. They become their own judgment. Then their own need for mercy saves them from the pride which goes with their demand for justice.

The phrase "... one by one they went away, the eldest first ... has a particularly human meaning. Did the eldest one have more personal failings to remember? Does age create a more sensitive conscience? Or perhaps there came to the eldest the realization that no man has a right to judge his brothers or his sisters. Maybe age helps us to recognize our common need for forgiveness. The loud voice does not bring us to the deeper spiritual truths, but the quiet words of Jesus does.

I have an old book in my library which has brought me much comfort and insight through the years of my life. It was published in 1908, but today it seems as fresh as morning. It is *Orthodoxy*, by G. K. Chesterton. That great Catholic layman wrote: "Remember that the Church went in specifically for dangerous ideas; she was a lion tamer. The idea of birth through a Holy Spirit, of the death of a divine being, of the forgiveness of sins, of the fulfillment of prophecies, are ideas which, anyone can see, need but a touch to turn them into something blasphemous or ferocious." He concludes this remarkable chapter with these words: "To have fallen into any one of the fads from Gnosticism to Christian Science would indeed have been obvious and tame. But to have avoided them all has been one whirling adventure; and in my vision the heavenly chariot flies thundering through the ages, the dull heresies sprawling and prostrate, the wild truth reeling—but erect" (pp. 184 and 186).

Amen! And nowhere is this paradoxical truth more apparent than in this incident at the temple, where justice and mercy are held together by the One who went beyond logic to bring us to truth.